OPTIONS TRADING

The Complete Guide to Learn Options Trading, Investing in Stocks, Financial Freedom, and Passive Income Streams.

Second Edition

RICHARD BLOOM

© Copyright 2020 - All rights reserved.

This document is geared towards providing exact and reliable information with regards to the topic and issue covered. The publication is sold with the idea that the publisher is not required to render accounting, officially permitted, or otherwise, qualified services. If advice is necessary, legal or professional, a practiced individual in the profession should be ordered.

From a Declaration of Principles which was accepted and approved equally by a Committee of the American Bar Association and a Committee of Publishers and Associations.

In no way is it legal to reproduce, duplicate, or transmit any part of this document in either electronic means or in printed format. Recording of this publication is strictly prohibited and any storage of this document is not allowed unless with written permission from the publisher. All rights reserved.

The information provided herein is stated to be truthful and consistent, in that any liability, in terms of inattention or otherwise, by any usage or abuse of any policies, processes, or directions contained within is the solitary and utter responsibility of the recipient reader. Under no circumstances will any legal responsibility or blame be held against the publisher for any reparation, damages, or monetary loss due to the information herein, either directly or indirectly.

Respective authors own all copyrights not held by the publisher.

The information herein is offered for informational purposes solely, and is universal as so. The presentation of the information is without contract or any type of guarantee assurance.

The trademarks that are used are without any consent, and the publication of the trademark is without permission or backing by the trademark owner. All trademarks and brands within this book are for clarifying purposes only and are the owned by the owners themselves, not affiliated with this document.

Table of Contents

Introduction 9
Chapter 1: Market Basics 13
  Traders and Orders 13
Chapter 2: Brokers and Market Regulations 27
  Platforms 27
Chapter 3: 37
Trends/Ranges and Support/Resistance 37
  Trends and Ranges 37
  Support and Resistance 43
Chapter 4: Risk Management and Mindset 47
  Quantitative and Qualitative 47
  Mindset 53
Chapter 5: Covered Calls 59
  Strategy Implementation 59
Chapter 6: The Collar Trade 66
  Execution 66
Chapter 7: Vertical Call Spreads 73
  Bull Call Spread 73

Bear Call Spread	76
Chapter 8: Challenges with Option Trade	**80**
Trailing Stop	81
Partial Profit Booking at Targets	82
Partial Profit Booking for Customers	83
Profit Booking Temporal Property for Sellers	83
Profit Booking on Fundamentals	84
Averaging Up	85
All-Time Low Line	86
Chapter 9: Options Trading Strategies	**87**
The following are basic option methods for beginners	88
Buying Puts (Long Put)	90
Protective Place	93
Chapter 10: Profit Drivers	**98**
Financial Profit Drivers	98
Non-Financial Profit Drivers	99
Chapter 11: Option Greek Four Factors to Measure Risks	**105**
Key Takeaways	105
Understanding Option Contracts	106
Influences on an Option's Value	107
Call Options	109

The Greeks 111
Delta 111
Probability of Being Profitable 113
Delta and Directional Risk 114
Gamma 115
Theta 118
Vega 120

Chapter 12: Steps to Extend Your Option Trading Profits 122

Scanning for Patterns may be a Suckers' Play for Options Traders 123

How to Return Up With a Stock Watch List 126

The rule of thumb is 127

Chapter 13: Maximize Your Option Commerce Profits 129

Options Trading Mistake 1: Shopping for Out-Of-The-Money (OTM) Call Options 129

Options Trading Mistake 2: Misunderstanding Leverage 131

Options Trading Mistake 3: Having No Exit Arrangement 131

Options Trading Mistake 4: Not Being Receptive to New Methods 133

Options Trading Mistake 5: Trading Illiquid

Options 134

Mistake in Options Trading 6: Experiencing a Delay in Short Options 136

Options Trading Mistake 7: Failure to Issue out Upcoming Events... 137

Options Trading Mistake 8: Garment into Spreads . 138

Options Trading Mistake 10: Ignoring Index Options for Neutral Trades.. 141

Chapter 14: Psychological Brick Ways for Handling Losses 143

Dysfunctional Brick Ways... 143

Sound Brick Ways 144

The Bottom Line 145

Key Takeaways 146

Long-term Results.. 148

How Profitable Traders Create Cash 150

Conclusion 157

References 160

Introduction

Stocks, bonds, FX, derivatives, futures, options, CFDs….the list goes on and on and on. The financial world these days is diverse in nature and there is no limit to the number of vehicles you can use to make profits. Options are exactly one such instrument and come under the umbrella of derivatives.

Derivatives are instruments that are named thus because they literally derive their values from another financial instrument. Futures contracts, for example, are a derivative contract that promises a certain price of the underlying stock, or financial instrument, to be delivered at the date mentioned on the contract, regardless of the market price at the time of sale, or in the future.

Options work in a similar manner but there's more nuance to them than a futures contract and as such, options greatly reduce the risk associated with a lot of trading operations. However, and this is a huge caveat, you need to know how to use them.

Is it possible to make a million dollars trading options? Yes, of course, it is. Are you going to make a million dollars after reading this book? Most likely not. You see, a lot of beginners jump into trading expecting millions of untold riches and generally approach the whole discipline with ridiculous expectations.

Your trading operations are a business, and if any business could make its proprietors a million dollars with an investment of just a few thousand, you can bet no other form of business would ever exist, because what would be the point of them? A very good trader, and I mean one of the best in the world, will expect to make twenty percent returns on their capital. Warren Buffett has averaged twenty percent on his business since inception and he's considered the greatest businessman ever. So, yeah, if you're expecting a hundred percent per month, you need a reality check.

These numbers will sound low if your expectations are unrealistic. However, trading is wonderful in that it is one of those rare businesses where if you can follow correct principles, as I'll show you in this book, money and capital will find you once you establish a decent track record.

Your own money is not the only source of capital. These days, there are a number of capital-sourcing programs for retail traders such as fundeseeder, psyquation, and darwinex that function as a virtual, fully audited track record which institutional investors can review and invest in. So, don't be discouraged by thinking your thousand dollar capital isn't going to grow soon. Trust the process and follow the principles, and capital will find you, no doubt.

Capital is another key issue for a lot of traders. Like every other business, trading requires a certain amount of capital for it to be worthwhile. Now, can you trade with a thousand dollars of capital? Sure, you can. You can also choose to walk from New York to LA instead of catching a flight when it comes down to it.

A lot of traders get hung up on the low barriers of entry trading provides and miss the point that low capital will only hamstring you in the long run and you'll end up spinning your wheels. In the United States, especially, it is not advisable to trade with less than $25,000, and I'll explain why in subsequent chapters.

If you do not have this much capital, my advice is simply not to trade. Focus on building your capital to this point and learning the correct mindset. Speaking of which, mindset and risk management do not get anywhere near the importance in any other trading book simply because explaining trading strategies, that is entry points, takes up a lot of time.

Here's the deal: developing entry strategies is easy. It is managing risk that is difficult. This is where options come in handy. They simply remove all aspects of risk management by defining it right at the start and all you have to do is to monitor your trade. Options strategies, quite simply, help you get out of your own way.

Successful "Options Trading" requires you to understand the basics first, and in this book, I've given you some readymade strategies you can use to profit immediately. To make these really work though, you will need to understand the concepts of risk and adopt the correct approach to trading.

While entire books can be written only on the subject of the mindset necessary for trading success, I have addressed this topic in just one chapter. This book will begin by giving you a basic layout of what goes on behind the scenes in the markets, followed by a primer on risk management, and then mindset. It is only after this that we will look at options trading strategies.

The reason for this is because the most important things need to be addressed first. Fix your mindset and profits will follow. Options are not a magic bullet for your trading results, especially if you happen to be struggling with another instrument already. If you're a rank beginner, options don't require any special experience, but do beware that you're not exempt from following risk and mindset principles.

So, having said all that, let's dive in and peel back the curtain to reveal what goes on behind the scenes in the markets.

Chapter 1: Market Basics

Most of us interact with the market via financial TV channels or on the internet via a few stock charts. Both of these sources, while excellent sources of information, present a very distorted view of the markets, unfortunately. They always seem to convey some sense of panic or euphoria, with nothing in between.

Hollywood doesn't help either. Traders are almost always shown trading stocks by screaming obscenities at one another, and if the glorified used car salesman who dubbed himself "The Wolf of Wall Street" is to be believed, drugs and other stimulants are quite common.

None of these depictions are necessary for success, even though one might choose to approach things in this manner.

Traders and Orders

Fire up any trading terminal and the first thing you see is a video game-like layout with flashing numbers, green or red, and a number of lines and graphs signifying who knows what. All these lines and flashes of light signify one thing and one thing only--the actions of other traders.

There are all kinds of traders in the market, all the way from retail traders, who don't know their stocks from their toes, to institutional traders trading on behalf of a large bank or a hedge fund. There are speculators and investors, macro investors and high-frequency traders, and quantitative traders. The market is like its own solar system with all kinds of strategies forming the various planets within it.

The equivalent of the sun, the center of it all, would be "price". Price is what ultimately everyone is haggling over, and when an agreement is reached, you see a flash of red or green on your screen. Price charts depict the course of price in certain time intervals. For example, a daily chart shows the progression of price for an entire market session, or in the case of FX, an entire twenty-four hours.

Similarly, a fifteen-minute chart shows the movements of price every fifteen minutes and a five-minute chart every five minutes. There are different ways of representing price so let's take a look at these.

Price Charts

There are three kinds of price charts you will encounter in the markets. The first is the one which provides the least amount of information and is generally used by popular media like TV channels and so on. Perhaps there's a connection there, but anyway, this chart is the simple line chart which depicts price as a line, going up or down with the percent change next to it in either red or green.

Plotting this line is simple enough. You place a dot for the level at which price closed the previous day and connect it to the dot which symbolizes market close or current price at a given moment, and you have a line which is either above, below, or at the same level. This is what the percent change measures. The line chart looks pretty and provides easy conclusions for laymen and as such, you will not find any trader ever looking at price represented this way.

The next kind of chart, which is a huge improvement over the humble line chart, is the American bar chart. I'm calling this American because it is usually found only Stateside and not so much around the world. The representation of price in a bar chart is shown in Figure 1 below.

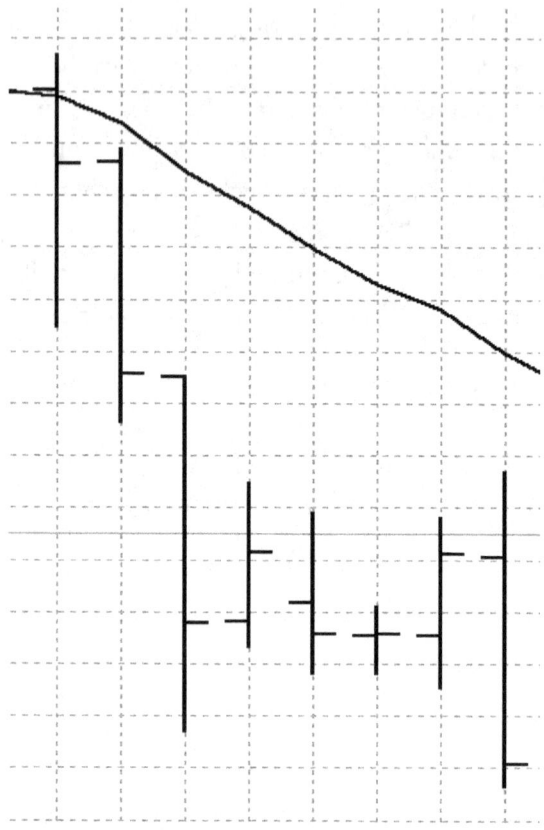

Figure 1: A bar chart (MetaTrader 4, 2015)

Each bar in this image represents price action for a given interval. So, if these bars were on a daily chart, one bar represents what price did during that entire day. If it's a sixty-minute chart, it represents hourly price action and so on. Let's break this down more.

The vertical line represents the range of price movement.

Thus, the top of this line is the high that price achieved during this interval and the lowest point is the low during the same interval. The larger the vertical line is, the greater the range with which price moved. The notch on either side of the vertical line signifies the open and close, with the open on the left and close on the right.

Bars are fantastic this way because they don't need any special color or design characteristics. By just looking at the notches, we can see whether price increased during the interval or decreased. If the notch on the right is higher than the one on the left, then the price increased, and if the one on the left is higher, then the price decreased during the time interval.

The relative positions of the open and close notches to the high and low provide excellent information with regards to the price action during the session. For example, a close that's far above the low and the high, that is with a tail, signifies buying pressure that overcame selling pressure. The same applies if a wick exists to the top.

Bars, despite the amount of information they provide, do have their shortcomings. For one, they're not the most graphically communicative. When seen in a cluster, the bars do tend to blend in with one another. The most informative way of communicating price action is "candlesticks" and this is what most professional traders use.

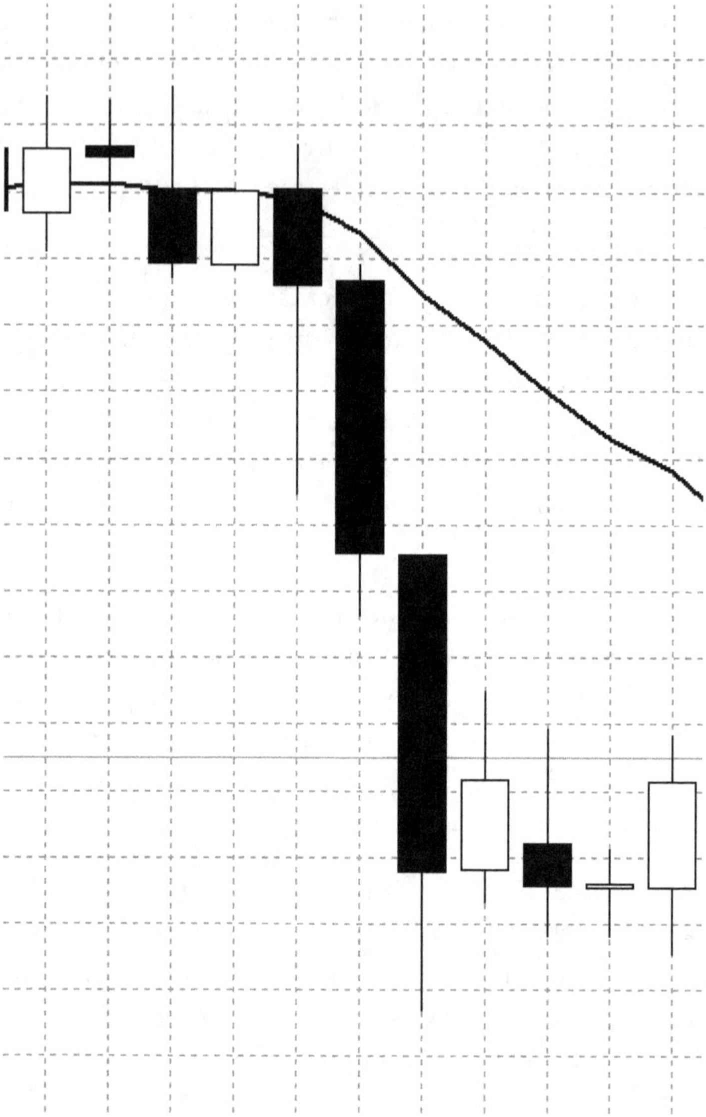

Figure 2: Candlestick chart

Candlesticks, or candles as they're called, have the same information as bars do. They communicate the open, close, high low, and the range within which price moved during the given time interval. The difference is that the body of the candle is a far more graphic representation of the range. Aside from communicating the extent of the price range, the color of the bar informs us whether price decreased or increased during the time interval.

Bullish bars or bars whose close is higher than the open, have a different color from bearish ones, that is bars where the close is below the open. The colors can be chosen by the trader and conventionally, charting platforms assign the color red to bearish bars and blue to bullish ones. In this book, I'll be signifying bullish bars with white bodies and bearish candles with black bodies.

Candlesticks provide an instant snapshot of price action and they can be traded individually via patterns. The highs and the lows are represented by the wicks on either side of the body and the size of the body, wick size, and location with respect to the candle body form a pattern which can be used to draw conclusions.

Let's look at a few patterns that will help you get up and running quickly.

Candlestick Patterns

The first pattern that will prove extremely useful to you is the inside bar. This is shown in figure 3.

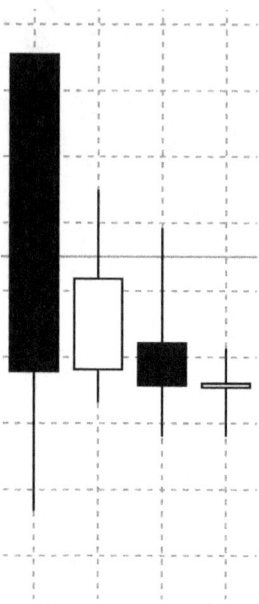

Figure 3: Inside bar cluster (MetaTrader 4, 2015)

The pattern is comprised of two bars, with the one on the right lying within the range of the body of the bar on the left. Now, it isn't fully necessary for the smaller bar's wicks to be completely within the bigger bar's body. It's far more important that the order flow characteristics of this pattern is understood.

Inside bars are a continuation pattern which indicates that the current market situation will persist. Thus, if the market is in a bull trend and then price hesitates sideways and forms an inside bar, you can bet that the original trend will continue. This is true of bullish and bearish trends.

The only market situation where you should not be trading is when inside bars are in ranges. If you're not familiar with what trends and ranges are, this is something I'll address shortly in a later chapter. However, for now, just remember that inside bars, and indeed all price patterns, are meant to be used in certain environments.

The next useful candlestick pattern is the pin bar which is illustrated in figure 4.

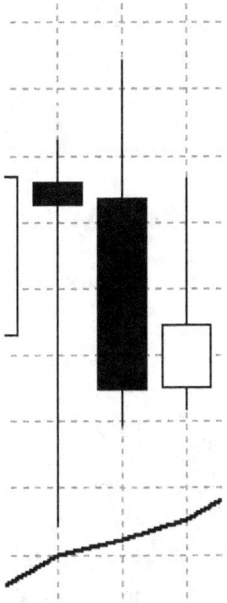

Figure 4: Pin bars on either side of a bearish bar (MetaTrader 4, 2015)

The pin bar is a single bar formation and signifies a reversal. Despite being a reversal pattern, the best way to trade this for a beginner is to do so with trend. This means that when price moves in a small sideways pattern once it takes a breather in a trend, look out for a pin bar to signify the end of the sideways pattern and resumption of the trend. Figure 5 illustrates how this works.

Figure 5: Pin bar provides continuation signal
(MetaTrader 4, 2015)

The pin bar is characterized by a small body and a wick or tail above or below the body. Generally speaking, it is preferable to have the wick or tail's length to be at least thrice the size of the body. Again, don't get caught up in measuring things, just understand the underlying trade mechanics.

Wicks and tails happen when traders reject a certain price level strongly. This is even more significant if the body is small because it indicates that the original downward or upward movement was strong but then it was rejected by an even stronger movement that produces the wick or the tail. When such a pattern occurs at or near an important support or resistance level, it is about as blaring a sign the market will ever give you as to which direction it is about to move in.

"Support and Resistance" is discussed in detail in a separate chapter but in case you're unfamiliar with these, they're essentially important order flow levels where traders draw lines in the sand and defend it. S/R is an important skill set for you to master in order to trade successfully.

The last candlestick pattern that will prove itself extremely useful is the climaxing pattern. The climax occurs at the very end of a bullish or bearish move and is accompanied by what can be best termed as "exaggerations". The sizes of the bars involved are exaggerated far beyond the usual size in the trend; the volumes peak massively and the rebound of the climax is fast and sharp as well.

Climaxes are counter-trend trades and generally, I don't recommend beginners trade in this manner but it is actually a simple trade to take once you learn how to spot a climax. The reason it is simple is because you don't need to worry about S/R or any other market events.

Figure 6: Bear trend ends in a climax

Climaxes are also referred to as exhaustive movements and are characterized by massive trend bars accompanied by huge volumes. The bar sizes and volumes are not just larger than ordinary but far larger, almost twice the magnitude. It is important that you look for this extreme exaggeration since it indicates that weak with trend players, in other words--the uninformed public, has entered the market and are jumping onto the bandwagon right when it's too late.

What follows as climax is either a sideways movement which eventually leads to a trend reversal or a sharp counter-trend bounce that is then followed by a meandering sideways movement. This is advantageous and we'll see how to trade these sideways movements when talking about ranges in a later chapter.

Climaxes are excellent in terms of the ROI they offer on your time as well. Given the pace with which price moves counter-trend post the climax, you'll earn your profits soon. From a rice environment perspective, you want to look for these near the end of trends and not in ranges. Climaxes give birth to ranges and don't occur within them.

This covers the main points in terms of the market basics you need to know and understand. The key lesson to take away from all this is that the market is just a giant collection of orders being matched with one another and that these orders reflect sentiment.

Sentiment is not always logical but is always chaotic. However, over a long enough period, sentiment leaves patterns which repeat themselves more often than not. By ensuring we can spot such patterns and recognize the odds inherent in them, we can trade successfully. This will be covered in the chapter on risk management and mindset.

For now, remember that you don't necessarily need indicators or special tools to trade the market. Indicators are simply derived from price and as such, the price chart has all the information you need. Traders tend to rely on indicators because the seeming complexity of the price chart scares them.

Options take away a lot of this problem but before we dive into options' basics, it is important to get to know that most important person in your trading business--your broker. In addition, you will also need to learn about the laws surrounding trading and why it is important to be well-capitalized.

All this and more is covered in the next chapter.

Chapter 2: Brokers and Market Regulations

The broker is usually the only person in the market who is guaranteed to make any money. Too many beginners place far too much importance on the broker and the functions they perform. This is not to say that the broker is unimportant, just that beginner traders tend to blame their broker for things that are really not the broker's fault.

In this chapter, we'll begin by looking at brokers and price charts, cover the basics of option quotes in most broking platforms and end with a word about market regulation.

Platforms

When it comes to brokerage services, you have two choices: discount or full service. Full-service brokers provide end to end options (service options that is, not the instrument) to help separate you from your money. This might sound cynical but is really just the nature of the brokerage business.

A broker's only duty is to execute your trades. It is not to provide investment advice or trade ideas, neither is it to provide research reports on the market and express opinions that can guide your trading decisions. Do not make the mistake of assuming that just because a broker is an old institution and has many different lines of business, such as wealth management solutions and so on, that they are better than the rest.

For this reason, discount brokers are your best choice since they tend to reduce their focus to just what a broker is really supposed to do. They will do this at lower commissions and will remove a lot of the fancy accessories like having a personal relationship manager or a phone hotline for you to phone in your trades.

To clarify, I'm not saying that you should never invest your money in the markets with the big banks. If you have access to a good financial planner and they recommend certain services, go for it. My point is that trading is a separate business and you should not make this a part of your retirement plan. Rather, you need to treat trading profits as a nice bonus.

Having this mindset will remove the need for you to make money and will remove a lot of the emotions that will sabotage your trading efforts. For example, doubling down on losing trades and taking profits too early are telltale signs of the fact that you feel the need to earn some money to pay for your living expenses from trading.

Trading should be conducted as a business and your broker is much like a supplier if you were running a grocery store.

Options Trading

You need a decent level of service but the costs need to make sense for you to turn a profit. If a washing powder supplier begins telling a grocery store owner how to price the products or what margins to charge the customer, you can bet the supplier will be told to shut his mouth post-haste.

However, people seem to expect this same nature of investment advice from a broker. The more you trade, the more the broker earns and this conflict of interest escapes a lot of beginners. The long and short of all this is, choose a discount broker and make your own trading decisions. Do not ask for investment advice or any advice at all from your broker. It just puts both of you in an uncomfortable position.

When it comes to trading options, you need to have the basics in terms of trading platforms. These are a price chart with real-time data and the ability to superimpose indicators on them. Live option chain information (I'll shortly explain what an option chain is) and metrics such as open interest and market event news and timings.

Every broker out there has these fundamental features, so simply choose the one which has the lowest commissions and good rates. It is advisable to have more than one broker once your account size builds up to over fifty thousand dollars, just to distribute your risk more evenly. Until then, sticking with one broker is fine.

Price Quotes

When it comes to price quotes, you need to be aware of three components: the Bid, the Ask, and the LTP. Let's start with the LTP first. LTP stands for Last Traded Price and is the price you will see on the ticker board and on a lot of financial media. This price is simply the last negotiated price and reflects the trade price of the latest trade.

Do not make the mistake of thinking this is the market price. In reality, there is no market price but more of a band within which price trades. This band is called the "spread". Instruments that are traded heavily, that is, have huge demand and supply, will have a low spread and less liquid, or thinly traded instruments will have a large spread.

Spread implies a gap between two points and these two points are the bid and the ask. When you fire up your trading platform, you'll notice that price is quoted in a box as two numbers, the bid and the ask. The ask is the price that is being offered to you on the market in case you wish to buy the instrument. The bid is the price you have to pay in order to sell it.

The gap between the two is the spread. As you can imagine, the spread size doesn't always remain the same. In periods of high volatility, that is when there is a massive demand or supply that occurs suddenly causing huge swings in the bid and the ask, the spread will increase in size and might also narrow suddenly.

This usually occurs during important news announcements or during other events such as interest rate announcements and so on. The bid and the ask will jump up and down by many greater points of magnitude than usual and this will manifest itself as major spikes and troughs in the price chart, or wider candles and gaps in between them. Figure 7 illustrates what a gap is.

Figure 7: A gap in price bars (MetaTrader 4, 2015) (MetaTrader 4, 2015)

Either way, the point is that you should be aware that the LTP is not the prevalent market price but is just a reflection of where the spread was. Where the spread is now depends on the current volatility within the market. It might be close to the LTP or it might be far away. As a beginner, it is best to stick to instruments that have low volatility and high liquidity; in other words, instruments that have a low spread and where the LTP is usually a good reflection of where the spread currently is.

Options prices are quoted in the same manner and usually, an option quote has all the information you need to know contained right within it.

Options Basics

An option is a contract that is struck between two parties, a buyer and a seller or writer. As mentioned earlier, options are derivative contracts and can be derived from an underlying stock or FX pair. The writer of the option agrees, when writing an option to or selling an option to the buyer, to buy or sell the underlying stock at a given price called the "strike price" before a certain date, called the "expiry date".

The buyer can choose either to exercise or not to exercise the option before the expiry date. In return, the buyer pays a small amount, called a premium, to the option writer/seller. Thus, when you check the price of an option on a stock, you'll see the spread indicating the premium prices at which you can buy or write the option. This premium is dependent on the underlying stock price but is not actually the same.

Options Trading

Options contracts come in two forms, "Calls" and "Puts". A call is where the writer agrees to sell the underlying stock to the buyer at the strike price, and a put is where the writer agrees to buy the underlying from the buyer. In other words, if you buy a call, you can buy the stock at the strike price and if you buy a put, you can sell the stock at the strike price.

As an example: Let's say you like the look of AMZN and think that the stock is going to increase in price. In such a case, buying a call with a strike price that is close to current price is a good bet. If the stock rises in price, the option will move into the money (that is, it will make you money if you exercise it) and you can buy AMZN at the lower strike price by exercising the option.

Similarly, if you think AMZN is going to decrease in price, you buy a put and when it does decrease, you sell AMZN at the higher strike price by exercising the put and buy it back at the lower market price to make a profit. What happens, if AMZN doesn't move in your favor though?

Well, this is where options are great. If your option is not in the money by the expiration date, you can simply let it go. You will lose only the premium you paid for the option when you bought it. AMZN's stock price is currently around $1889. If you wish to buy a hundred shares, it's going to cost you a cool $188,900. However, the 1850 put expiring on August 2nd costs just $52.03. Each option contract represents 100 shares of underlying stock so you would pay $5203 for control over one hundred AMZN shares.

Contract, both puts and calls, exist for all combinations of prices and expiry dates. Thus, you will have a call and put option for $1800 expiring this month, next month, the month after and so on. Usually, contracts are thinly traded, i.e. illiquid, beyond expiry dates two months out.

This collection of contracts is called the options chain and is simply the list of premiums for every combination of option type (call/put), expiry date (this month, next month etc.) and strike price ($180o, $1810, $1790 etc.). As mentioned previously, when exercising an options contract will make you money, it is said to be in the money. In the case of puts, this is when the stock price is less than the strike price and in the case of calls, it is when the strike price is below the market price.

In your trading platform, you will see a label termed "options chain" and this will display a table of strike prices for a given date for both calls and puts.

Market Regulations

Trading options involves borrowing money or stock, also called "margin". When you decide to exercise a put, you're borrowing stock from someone else, which the broker has to arrange and you will need to pay interest on that borrowing. Thus, the SEC and FINRA, who are the regulators of the stock and options markets, stipulate that brokers require a minimum investment amount in the trading account.

Now, there are usually five levels of risk, when it comes to options trades as defined by brokers. The strategies identified in this book will put you somewhere between levels one to three, depending on the broker. For such levels, you can expect a minimum balance of around five thousand to ten thousand dollars.

Furthermore, you also have to contend with the pattern day trade rule. A pattern day trader is someone who executes four or more trades within five business days (Chen, 2019). Thus, if you buy and sell two options contracts between Monday to Friday, you are a pattern day trader. FINRA stipulates that such accounts must have a minimum of twenty-five thousand dollars as a balance.

This is why I mentioned this amount as being the minimum amount of capital you must have if you wish to trade options. Now, is it absolutely necessary to have this amount? Could you trade with less? Sure, you could. However, you cannot enter or exit your trades at will. Remember, every trade execution is counted, not just your entries.

Trading is not an exact science where you'll say that you'll always exit your trades after a week. This is simply handicapping yourself and will slow your progress. Using the earlier example, it's a bit like deciding to walk to LA from New York because you can't afford a flight. It's better to save up and buy a ticket than to walk all the way that will cost you more in the long run.

There are a number of experts out there who have tons of YouTube videos explaining how you can avoid the PDT tag and still trade. All I'll say that such advice is a sure sign of a con artist. Be wary if you do choose to follow such people.

Now that we've looked at the capital you'll need and understood which regulations govern you, let's take a look at some technical analysis basics.

Chapter 3: Trends/Ranges and Support/Resistance

Unlike other books on trading, I'm not going to list out every technical indicator out there and pretend that these constitute trading strategies. Why? Well, it's far easier to simply look at the price chart and make your decisions there when it comes to trading options.

You can use indicators, but every indicator out there is simply derived from price charts and market mechanics. Isn't it far better to interpret things at the source than to superimpose something else on top of it and try to draw conclusions? The source of all market information is the order flow and we can interpret order flow but looking at the presence of trends and ranges and secondly, via support and resistance levels.

Trends and Ranges

Market price action can be classified into two states: trends and ranges. Trends are when the market is headed in a definite direction and ranges are when it is going sideways. Trends have greater profit potential as you can imagine, but can be difficult for beginners to trade.

This is because the price is constantly moving away from levels and it can be difficult to spot an ideal entry point. By the time you think you've spotted a good entry point, the price has already moved well beyond it or has simply not pulled back to where you think it was going to.

This is why I always recommend that beginners learn ranges inside and out and build some skill trading them first. By trading ranges, you will establish a baseline profit level which can then absorb the missed trades or losses you will incur by trading trends.

Identifying ranges is fairly straightforward as we'll see next.

Range Identification and Profiting

Figure 8: A Range (MetaTrader 4, 2015)

Figure 8 illustrates a classic example of a range. As you can see, looking left to right, the price is moving sideways. A range will always have easily identifiable boundaries at the top and bottom. In this case, we can see the peaks that price makes from a pretty stable boundary on top and a relatively clear one at the bottom.

Now, this is a point where most beginners trip themselves up. You cannot expect the price to line up exactly in a horizontal line. In fact, the price will almost never do this. Thus, when trying to make support and resistance zones or range boundaries, which are S/R zones themselves, always look for a zone.

This is why in figure 8, you can see four lines, two at the top and two at the bottom, which signify the upper boundary zone and lower boundary zone respectively. Note that price pierces this zone multiple times to the top and bottom. However, when marking the zone, we are most concerned with the areas where the majority of price action lines up, not every single point.

Thus, as this range progresses, we have a very simple and straightforward template for making profits. As long as the price is in between the boundaries, we will short the top and go long off the bottom. In other words, we can sell the instrument when it reaches the upper boundary and buy the instrument when it reaches the lower boundary. To make a profit, we can choose to ride price all the way to the other boundary or take an earlier profit.

If you're trading directionally, as in the previous paragraph, you will need to place your stop-loss orders beyond the zones. However, with options, we don't need to worry about such things. I'll later be explaining the collar trade which will eliminate all risks in such situations and is a non-directional trade. However, you can trade directionally using options as well and buy a put at the top of the range and buy a call at the bottom.

Ranges typically occur at the end of long trends and prior to the start of one. These types of ranges tend to have redistribution going on within them; in other words, the buyers and sellers are trading places of power in the market. We'll see why this happens in the next section.

Either way, you can safely trade the tops and bottoms of ranges that occur at the end of trends and within trends; it is safer to trade in the direction of the trend using the range as an entry point. For example, in a bear trend, shorting the top of the range in anticipation of a move lower, and the trend continuing is a great example of an entry into the larger trend.

Often, you will see a trend on a high timeframe, say the daily timeframe, go sideways for a bit. This sideways movement, on the lower timeframes, usually the five minutes of fifteen minutes, prints as a range and you can either trade this range or use it as an entry point to enter the higher timeframe trend.

Whatever you do, stay away from the middle of the range

since this is where the order flow, that is trader presence, is the least and price flow is unpredictable. Always trade from areas where order flow is the highest.

Trend Trading

I will reiterate here that you need to practice and master trading ranges before trading trends. You need to understand order flow mechanics in greater depth before being able to trade trends successfully. In terms of trading options, however, you need not fully learn this before beginning to make money since the strategies I will illustrate later are market neutral, that is to say, you'll make money no matter which way the market moves.

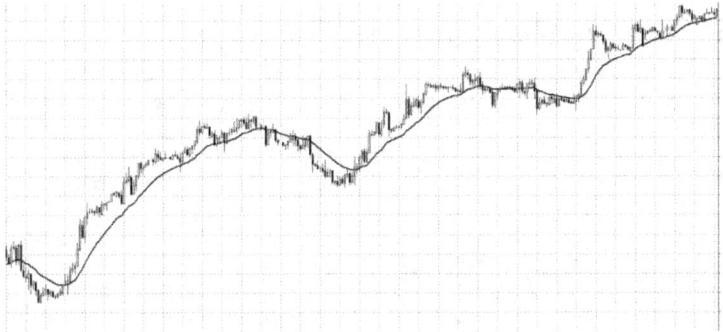

Figure 9: An uptrend (MetaTrader 4, 2015)

Figure 9 illustrates a long bullish trend. Notice how price doesn't simply move upwards at a constant angle but goes up, sideways and even down on some occasions before eventually moving upwards. Trends are fundamentally the result of one set of traders, representing one side of the market, overpowering the other side of the market and thus pushing the price in a given direction.

As the other side pushes back, a struggle ensues and much like a battle, this sequence is a series of attacks, strategic retreats and defeats. The ultimate aim for both sides is to dominate the market and the stronger a side is, the steeper the price curve.

Notice how on the left of figure 9, the price is almost vertical. This is because there are no sellers present and the buyers push forward with impunity. However, as the trend progresses, the angle of attack with which the price moves forward becomes shallower until price moves sideways, dips back to a deep level where buyers reassert their dominance and then push prices higher.

Now, if this were a book on directional trading, I would go into identifying order flow mechanics and how to determine whether the buying pressure or selling pressure is faring. However, when it comes to trading options, all you really need to be able to do is to identify trends and ranges, especially the latter. While it is good to build your skills and identify the strength of the current trend, it isn't necessary for you to trade options successfully.

Overall, understand that ranges result from the order flow where both the bulls and bears are equally strong and trends from order where one side is stronger than the other.

Of far greater importance is your ability to draw proper support and resistance levels.

Support and Resistance

"Support and Resistance" is quite misunderstood when it comes to trading. A lot of traders, sadly even advanced ones who should know better, treat S/R as a bunch of lines on a chart. The reality is that S/R is the biggest imprint of order flow and provides the best entry points into the market.

By best, I mean entry points where risk is as low as possible for a given reward. The risk of entering at a strong S/R level is low because this is where you will find the greatest support from like-minded traders who will push the price in your favor. Reading S/R and entering correctly is thus simply figuring out the intentions of the market and joining the dominant order flow at the right moment.

Some key forms of S/R are as follows:

1. Swing highs and lows
2. Prior areas on a chart where price reacted significantly
3. Dynamic S/R like the 20EMA or Fibonacci levels
4. Range boundaries.

We've already seen how price can repeatedly ping off range boundaries and provide excellent entry points. Let's look at the other three and see how they work.

Major and Minor Levels

Figure 10: S/R levels, minor and major (MetaTrader 4, 2015)

Figure 10 illustrates how powerful S/R entries can be. The picture looks a bit crowded at first but perfectly illustrates the different kinds of S/R levels you will see.

First off, from an overall market perspective, we're looking at a portion of the price action which shows the end of a bear trend, a range where orders are redistributed and the start of a bull trend. This is on the four-hour timeframe, so each bar represents price action for four hours, and the instrument is the FTSE 100 which is the UK stock market index.

If you look at the horizontal lines on top, they signify the top of the range. Now, this range isn't particularly clean but the level is valid because, as you can see from the circles on the left, price clearly is being pushed down by the bears at this level. Eventually, the bulls don't manage to bring it back here until much later, to the right of the chart.

As the price re-approaches the top of the range on the right, strangely, the bears don't mount any resistance and a short at this level would have resulted in a loss. However, look at what happens next. Price goes past the level, forms a pin bar on it, signifying the continuation of the uptrend, and then dips back into the level to use it as support to move further on. Thus, we can see that the top of the range served as resistance first and then turned into support. If you were looking to trade with the trend, once the range broke, the prior top of the range was an excellent entry point.

Similarly, the triangles illustrate the price behavior at the bottom of the range. Notice how the bear trend exhausts itself at the first triangle on the left. While the retest of this level on the right is unclean; traders still remember this level and price uses it as support to pingback upwards.

These two levels, the prior range boundaries, are the major S/R levels on this chart. The greater the number of hits on a level and the stronger the reactions from that level, the greater a level's importance.

As price moves its way back up from the second triangle on the right, we encounter an example of a minor resistance level at the two squares. Here, the price pulls back and forms a minor swing high at the first square. It then dives down and then rushes past the swing high, and uses it as support on its way up.

Price here behaves much like it will shortly do when it will break the range boundary on top. However, the squares are a minor level and not a great entry point because at the moment they occur, the price is still stuck in a range. This level is far away from the bottom and order can be unpredictable. We could have gone down a few timeframes and seen if there was an opportunity there but not at this timeframe.

Next, we see a Fibonacci indicator next to the letter A. Notice how the price retraces to the 50% level of the Fibonacci and then moves back up. Well, this is another minor level for the same reasons as the squares. Price still hasn't broken out above the range and from a range perspective, this is not a good entry point.

If this had occurred during a strong trend, say right after it broke out of the range, then this minor level could have been taken as an entry point.

The lesson for you to understand is that levels exist everywhere but stick to major levels the majority of the time and use minor levels only when the force of the order flow is extremely dominant in your preferred direction.

Now that you have a basic understanding of S/R principles, it is time to move on and look at risk management and mindset.

Chapter 4: Risk Management and Mindset

We've now arrived at the most important things that will ensure your trading success: managing risk and having the right mindset to ensure success. Options are an excellent choice for trading precisely because of their ability to manage risk better. This is why professional traders choose to operate with them in more complex strategies.

In this chapter, we'll dive into the basics of risk management and then look at the beliefs you need to possess in order to be successful in the markets.

Quantitative and Qualitative

Risk management is both qualitative and quantitative. The quantitative bit is far easier to understand since it is just a matter of crunching numbers and monitoring a bunch of statistics with regards to your account. Now, if you were trading directionally, the number of metrics you need to monitor is enormous.

Thankfully, when it comes to options, you only need to track a few. Let's take a look at these.

Risk per Trade

More than anything else, it is your risk per trade that determines your success. Common wisdom is to not risk more than two percent of your capital per trade and in the case of options trading, this is correct. Directional trading requires you to risk far less than this in order to be successful.

The true measure of a good trader is how consistent they are in risking the same percentage of their account on each and every trade. A lot of beginners get on a winning streak at times and then start playing loose with this, only to be hit by a big loss that wipes out all their prior gains.

There is a school of thought that proposes that risking a fixed amount per trade, as opposed to a fixed percentage, is a better model. Now, you must understand that entire books can be written on risk management and I don't really have the space here to fully explain statistically why this is a bad idea. Suffice to say that, risking the same amount will bring you greater gains per trade and exaggerate your winning streaks but will do the same to your losses.

What's more, thanks to your losses being exaggerated, you'll have to constantly keep making more and more gains to simply breakeven and this will wipe out your account pretty soon since the basic math of all this is against you. Remember, you can't precisely predict the outcome of most trades in advance. Thus, it's best to risk the same percentage of your account every trade.

Win Percent

The win percentage of your strategy, that is the number of times you make money, is one half of an important measure that determines whether you'll make money or not. Usually, thanks to the way we've been brought up and have had UR performances measured in school, we chase the highest win percentages, thinking ninety percent is better than forty.

Well, in academia, this is true. However, in the chaotic world of the markets, this is far from the case. Making money on a trade is not about being right. You can be right about the markets and still lose money in the long run. This is best explained after we look at the second half of the equation.

Average Win Percent

Your average win percent is the amount of money you win on average, when you do make money, expressed as a percentage of your account or as a multiple of the amount you risk per trade on average. So, if you risk R per trade, which might be 2% of your account, and if you make 4% on a win on average, you will make 2R per win.

The average win percent and the win percent together determine whether you'll make money or not. So out of ten trades, if you win two, a win rate of twenty percent, and your average win is 2R, you will not make money. This is because your eight losses will cost you 8R and your wins will only amount to 4R. This is a net loss of 4R.

However, if you make 5R on average per win, you will make money with a twenty percent win rate. In this case, your losses will add up to 8R as previously but your wins will add up to 10R, giving you an overall profit of 2R. If you risk two percent of your account, this is a profit of 4% over ten trades.

Now if you manage to take two hundred trades over the course of a year, you'll be making 80% in a year. This is precisely what professional traders do make and it takes an extraordinarily high level of skill to hit such numbers. My point is that your profitability is determined by both numbers, not just a single one.

As you can see, it is perfectly possible to make money by being 'right' just twenty percent of the time. In a regular academic examination, this will guarantee your failure, but in the markets, it's just one half of an equation.

Strategy Evaluation

This gives us an excellent method of figuring out the profitability of strategies. If a strategy has a low win percent but high average win percent, it is perfectly valid to implement it, instead of trying to simply chase strategies that have high win percentages. For example, if you have the previously described strategy and another one with a

90% win rate but only a 0.5R average win percent.

Over two hundred trades, the previous strategy makes 80% but this strategy, which is correct 90% of the time, will make you 35% over the same number of trades. So, which is the better strategy? The one where you have more losses or the one where you have more wins? Clearly, asking which one has more wins or loses is missing the point.

So, don't blindly chase high win rates or strategies that claim you won't lose even a single trade. Such strategies don't exist unless you run a hedge fund focused on HFT front running strategies, in which case, you might have run into this book by mistake. For the rest of us, evaluating both the win percentage and the average win size as a function of the percent risk per trade is what determines whether or not a strategy is good.

Qualitative Risk

Let's say you settle down in front of your television on the weekend and switch on the TV to catch your favorite game. You're fully prepped and have your TV and assorted accessories set just so. Your friends have come over as well and all in all, it's a great atmosphere. There's just one problem: your team's star athlete, the one on whom the result of the game hinges, has turned up to the game hungover.

Now, it isn't unheard of such things to happen in pro sports, but when it does happen, you can imagine the reaction that follows. The athlete is roundly criticized as a buffoon, rightly so, and the sports media have a field day debating where he's about to be traded to next. We instinctively understand that preparation is the key to success and turning up hungover is hardly good preparation.

Yet, how many of us sit down to trade after having just walked in from work? We're tired and frustrated from whatever is going on in that world and think we can simply waltz in and make money in the markets. The very same markets that are full of professionals who make a living from it and are responsible for the management of many millions and billions.

Do you seriously think anyone can be successful trading this way? Do you think trading is simply a matter of learning the right strategies and then implementing it with the snap of a finger? If so, this is an indicator that your mindset is incorrect and that you don't understand what trading risk management involves.

Make no mistake; you will need to prepare and have your wits fully about you as you sit down to trade. You cannot afford any distractions like checking your smartphone or trying to wing something at the last minute. You need good sleep and need to exercise and eat well.

This is why I called the adrenaline-filled, coked-out atmosphere of trading floors in movies unrealistic because it is impossible to trade this way. A lot of beginners get seduced by this 'devil may care' type of depiction and try to do the same when it comes to their own hard-earned money. Needless to say, this results in a quick wipeout and the ones who will take their money are the traders who have prepared themselves.

You need to follow a specific mental and physical routine prior to operating in the markets. Meditation and other mental calming techniques are a great idea and will enable you to see things clearly, as they are. Also, avoid trading when things are not going well for you with your regular life.

There's no rule that says you have to trade each and every day of the year. Take adequate time to reflect on your skills and practice them well. Practice them so well that you know them by heart. The live market is not a place for you to be questioning whether the signal is valid or not. You simply need to pull the trigger and execute.

Sometimes, despite our best intentions, we fail to follow our plans. This is an indication that the problem is not so much with our technical strategy or risk but with our mindset.

Mindset

Here's a fun fact for you: Our brains are not biologically wired for us to trade successfully. This is why close to ninety percent of traders washout within a year of opening their accounts at brokerages (Tradecity Trading Academy, 2019). The good news is that our brains are learning machines and we can teach ourselves the way to success.

The biggest hurdle we face is our in-built negativity bias. The negativity bias is a part of our survival mechanism that gives greater priority to things that are harmful to us than things that give us pleasure. Thus, you are more likely to remember negative experiences than positive ones.

This is precisely why a lot of people chase high win rate systems irrespective of the strategy's overall profit potential. We are so conditioned to think that a high win rate means the avoidance of a bad performance that we forget to take into account how much we make per win on average.

This is also why executing a twenty percent win rate system is so difficult and requires a very high degree of skill. A twenty percent win rate implies losing eight out of ten trades. Most people cannot stomach losing two trades in a row, let alone being able to remain disciplined and absorb fifteen losers in a row (there is a 98% chance you will experience losing fifteen trades in a row if your strategy has a twenty percent win rate).

Simply reading that last sentence has probably convinced you that taking the less profitable strategy from the previous section is a good idea but this is giving in to the negativity bias. To trade successfully, you need to build a different mental model when it comes to trading.

The type of thinking that favors a high win rate system is excellent in an ordered setting, like an academic one. In such settings, you provide correct answers and you get rewarded. The market, however, is not ordered. It is chaotic. There are far too many players, too many trading systems and motivation to ever be able to make sense of it all.

Thus, you need to think in terms of odds and probabilities. Probabilistic thinking is what separates the professionals from the also-runs. Instead of being a gambler, you need to be the casino. This is actually a great example of how odds work, so let's run with it.

A casino knows the odds of each and every game on its floor. It knows that game X has odds of sixty percent, or that sixty percent of the time, the house wins and the gambler loses. Given this information, how does the house make money now? Well, first off, they fix the payout in proportion with the bet size.

The games that pay out a mega jackpot of over a million with low bet sizes usually have miserable odds, sometimes as much as ninety-eight percent stacked against the gambler. The game pays for itself via the number of hands people play. Even if the odd gambler wins the mega jackpot, it doesn't matter since the odds will play out and even themselves out over the long-run, and the house will make its money eventually.

This is why gamblers are plied with free drinks and comped rooms. Everything is set up to get you in a good mood and ignore the fact that you're flushing your money down the toilet and are stacking the odds against you the longer you play. This is why jackpot winners are immediately provided comped rooms and treated like royalty because it is in the casino's best interest to get them to gamble those winnings and increase the house's profits.

Hopefully, you're seeing the parallels with trading strategies now. Why should you care about a single trade? The results of a large number are what matter since the odds express themselves over a large sample size, not a small one. Thus, even if you do lose fifteen trades in a row, this means you're more likely to win the next one since the odds will even themselves out the longer you participate.

Thus, your main focus should be on maintaining the odds and the math that goes with it. Changing your risk percent every trade skews the math out of your favor since your average win sizes are now skewed. Your only focus should be to maintain the odds according to your calculations and focus on keeping your capital safe. The longer you keep your capital safe, the longer you play and the more you win.

A lot of us have toxic beliefs about money and becoming successful thanks to deeply ingrained programming. Perhaps we grew up poor or have a scarcity mindset when it comes to money. Use the below checklist to perform a mental checkup on yourself and see how you match up with those who have a proper and successful trading mindset.

Successful traders:

- Understand the odds of their system and know it inside out
- Are consistent with risk management
- Push the limits when it comes to expanding their skills
- Follow a structured and precise training regimen to develop their skills
- Recognize their negativity bias and limiting beliefs and implement techniques to combat this including:
    - Meditation
    - Visualization
    - Positive Affirmations
    - Breathing Techniques
- Are well capitalized and do not seek 'get rich quick' shortcuts
- Practice on paper first before going live
- Protect their capital at all costs

- Do not dream of Ferraris and yachts after a few wins on the trot
- Do not dream of despair and poverty after a few losses
- Do not need the market to validate their self-image
- Set their ego aside and follow their discipline and risk management rules

There are a number of books dedicated to helping you figure out how to get past your negative thoughts and to rewire your brain for success. Invest in yourself and commit to self-development. You will notice the benefits far beyond your trading results.

So now, having covered the basics, we're ready to learn options strategies which are low risk and will make you money. How well you execute them depends on your mental preparation and your dedication to your discipline.

So, without further ado, let's get into it!

Chapter 5: Covered Calls

The first options trading strategy we'll be looking at is the "Covered Call". This is an evergreen strategy and is perfect introductory strategy to options for those who are already used to buying stocks for investment purposes. To be clear, when I say investment, I mean holding a stock for a long timeframe based on fundamental factors of the stock such as revenue projections, earnings etc.

Investment of this kind is a very different beast from speculation and if you're planning on implementing the covered call with your day trading or swing trading positions, it's not going to work.

Strategy Implementation

The primary aim of the covered call is to reduce the cost of your stock holdings. For example, if you've purchased stock of say, Walmart, for $80 for your retirement account, your position is currently in a nice profit. As of the previous session, WMT is trading at $110.62; let's say you purchased two hundred shares for a total investment of $16,000.

If you could reduce your upfront investment in the stock, which is your cost basis, you stand to make a greater profit on this purchase. This is exactly what the covered call does. By writing a call option which is out of the money, you earn the option premium from the contract and thus increase your profit. In effect, you earn money while you're holding the position. Let's look at this via an example.

Key Points

Let's stick with WMT for our example. The current market price is $110.62 and your purchase price was $80. You have purchased two hundred shares. Your position is in a nice profit and you'd like to earn some additional money on this.

Covered calls require you to make a reliable estimate of the future price. Now, the thing to do is to not worry about an exact price projection but to see if the ballpark projection makes sense. If WMT is in a strong uptrend, then you will need to push your projected price further away than if it is currently in a big range. If you can see that counter-trend participation if becoming higher and the current trend in WMT is starting to go sideways, then you can risk a closer strike price for the call.

Let's say that WMT is in a situation where the trend is coming to an end. To earn a decent premium from writing the call, it is best to pick an option that expires at least two months from the current date. While this does expose you to price fluctuation over a longer term, if you can correctly read the market conditions, you will earn a higher premium.

For example, the call option expiring on August 2nd, which is one month away as of this writing, with a strike price of $130 is currently trading at one cent. In other words, if you were to write this option with this strike price, you'd earn just a cent from it. However, the September 20th 130 strike call is trading at six cents.

The longer-term option usually trades for a higher price because the stock has a greater chance of making it past the strike price. This is called the time premium within the option's price. If holding this position for this long is somewhat intimidating for you, you can choose a nearer-term option but you'll have to pick a closer strike price to earn the same premium.

For example, the August 2nd 125 strike call is selling for four cents. This is not only lesser in value but also has a much closer strike price. The only advantage you have is that the term is closer. However, even that is offset by the fact that the strike price is a lot closer to the current market price.

A lot of beginners make the mistake of wanting quick profits and end up losing their positions because of their impatience and greed. Here we can clearly see that the longer-term option is a better choice, provided our assumption of WMT ending its uptrend is true.

If WMT was in a strong uptrend showing no signs of

stopping, picking a strike price that is further away, say 150, would work better. Yes, you would earn a lesser premium but your long stock position will make a nice profit, so it's worth it. For now, let's stick to our original assumption of WMT ending its uptrend and write an option with a strike price of $130. All the numbers below are on a per-share basis.

Cost of stock purchase= $80

Income gained from writing 130 call= $0.06

If WMT stays below the 130 level till September 20th, our numbers now look like this.

Cost of stock purchase= Original cost- Income earned from option premium= 80-0.06= 79.40

Income earned on investment= premium earned/original cost=0.06/80= 0.07%

If the market price remains the same in September as it is now, that is at $110,

Profit based on initial cost price= 110-80= $30

Revised profit= 110-79.5= $30.5

If you hold your stock position long enough and if you keep writing covered calls successfully, you will keep earning income on the investment, along with any unrealized capital gains from the long position. In effect, it's a bit like owning a piece of real estate which appreciates in value but also provides you with rental income every month.

Boosting Gains and Other Scenarios

Keen-eyed readers will have noticed that the income return on the investment doesn't really amount to much. Well, this was just an example so the strike price is not optimized for maximum income. This is a key point to note here, especially for beginners because it deals with the mindset you ought to have when writing covered calls.

The covered call is not a 'get rich quick' strategy. In fact, nothing in this book is. The primary aim of the covered call is to enhance your long position's value and to keep reducing your cost basis over time. Thus, your primary aim with this strategy should be to supplement your capital gains with premium income that will accumulate over time.

The best-case scenario for such a position is that your long investment keeps increasing in size and meanwhile, thanks to the constant premium income, your cost basis keeps decreasing until it reaches a point where it is impossible for you to make a loss because your effective purchase price is extremely low.

To optimize this strategy, do not implement it until you've already accumulated enough unrealized gains on your long position. This way in the worst-case scenario, you will still be able to clear a profit. The worst-case scenario would be you picking a strike price that is not far enough away and the market price crosses it thereby leading to the call being exercised by the buyer.

In this case, you will need to sell your long position at the strike price and your position will be liquidated. If the stock keeps rising, you will miss out since you won't have a position anymore. A lot of beginner traders encounter this situation and end up losing their long position.

I'll say this once again: the covered call is a supplementary income-producing strategy. It is not a primary trading strategy. When you view it in this manner, you're more likely to pick strike prices on that basis of how likely the market is to cross that level instead of looking at it from a return on investment perspective.

The long position's gains should be viewed through the ROI lens, not the covered call's returns.

The best market conditions to deploy this strategy are found in a ranging market, a bearish one or even a mildly bullish one. During extremely bullish markets, stay away from this since it'll be tough for you as a beginner to get a feel for the right strike price.

Is there a formula or a method to pick strike prices? Well, there isn't unfortunately. The best way to pick strike prices is to evaluate upcoming resistance levels on the price chart. If you spot a strike price that is beyond a strong resistance level that the price has previously reacted to, it is a good bet that the price will react and spend time at that level again.

Thus, you need only be concerned with whether the breakout will occur prior to the call's expiry date, as opposed to whether it will ever break out at all like you would in a directional trade.

The covered call is an excellent strategy from a risk perspective as well if executed correctly. If you wait for a good profit cushion to be established on the long stock position prior to writing the call, there is virtually no condition in which you will take a loss.

Even if the call does get exercised, the strike price will be much higher than the cost price you paid. Of course, in the worst-case scenario, there is an opportunity cost, but my point is that there isn't any risk of a financial loss if executed correctly.

This concludes our look at the covered call. Next, we're going to look at collars which also comprise an excellent, zero risk strategy.

Chapter 6: The Collar Trade

Just like the covered call, the collar trade has three moving parts to it. It consists of a long stock position and a short, out of the money call just like the covered call strategy, and additionally a long put position.

By adding the long put position, you effectively cap the risk of this position no matter what the market does. This is something that no directional trading strategy will ever give you. Furthermore, the collar trade does not require any monitoring and pretty much runs on a little maintenance. Let's see how this works.

Execution

The first step to executing the collar trade is to establish a long stock position. This can be done as part of your usual investment activities, or unlike the covered call, even speculative ones. If you become bullish on a stock because of technical reasons but aren't fully sure which way it will go, hedging the risk of this position with a covered call will cap your maximum risk and give you a decent reward as well.

Once the long position is established, you need to buy an out of the money put, as close to the strike price as possible. Remember that buying a put gives you the right to sell the stock. Thus, if the market price decreases below the strike price of the put, you can sell the stock at the strike price and profit from the downward movement. Thus, the put protects you in case your bullish reasoning happens to be incorrect.

How far you choose to place your put is the key here. The distance between the strike price of the put and your stock purchase price is the loss you will have to take on the stock position if it declines. Thus, if you choose a put with a strike price just a few ticks below your stock purchase price, your risk on the stock purchase is extremely low. The farther away you go, the more you are risking.

The third step to executing a collar strategy is to write a call with an out of the money strike price, much like how you would do on a covered call. This price should be chosen with great care since it caps your maximum reward on the stock position. Thus, if you're quite bullish on the stock, you will need to pick a strike price that is farther out of the money than if you were just mildly bullish.

Writing a call will earn you a premium on this leg of the trade and will offset, by a little, the cost of buying the put to protect your downside. Thus, with your upside and downside capped, you don't need to worry about this trade anymore and are guaranteed a good profit whichever way the market moves, for an acceptable risk.

Let's further break this down via an example.

Running the Numbers

Sticking with WMT and its current market price of $110.62, we can see from its options chain that the September 110 put is selling for $3.45. This is the price we will have to pay if we choose this strike price for the put. Furthermore, let's say 130 is a good strike price for our call.

The premium for the September 130 call is 0.03$, which we will receive since we're writing the option. Thus, our numbers on this trade work out as:

Cost to enter per share= 110.62 (stock long position) + 3.45 (cost of put) - 0.03 (call premium received) = $114.04

Maximum risk or loss per share = Stock purchase price - Put strike price + cost of put - call premium = 110.62- 110 +3.45 - 0.03 = $4.04

Maximum profit per share = Call strike price - stock purchase price - cost of put + call premium = 130-110.62-3.45+0.03 = $15.96

This gives us a maximum reward to risk ratio of 3.95. If you were to cap your maximum risk at 2% of your account for this trade, your maximum reward will be close to 7% on just this trade. The worst-case scenario would be if the stock remained firmly in position until expiry thereby making you zero profit and only costing you money, which is a highly unlikely scenario, given that we're giving this trade three months to work.

With collars, the longer you give your trade time to work out, the better your prospects are of collecting the maximum reward, provided you've read the bullish conditions correctly. If you spot mildly bullish conditions, which are not likely to turn bearish, then picking a longer timeframe for the trade to work is a good idea.

Another way of increasing the profit potential of this trade is to choose a put that is out of the money. This increases your risk, but will give you a higher reward if you're confident enough in your bullish read.

Taking the previous example of WMT, if you choose to buy the September 100 put instead of the 110, your cost of the put is only $0.77 as of this writing. This means:

Cost to enter per share= 110.62 (stock long position) + 0.77 (cost of put) - 0.03 (call premium received) = $111.36

Maximum risk or loss per share = Stock purchase price - Put strike price + cost of put - call premium = 110.62- 100 +0.77 - 0.03 = $11.36

Maximum profit per share = Call strike price - stock purchase price - cost of put + call premium = 130-110.62- 0.77+0.03 = $18.64

As you can see, by choosing a put out of the money but keeping the call at the same level, you reduce your maximum reward risk ratio. The problem with this particular example is that the premium we receive for the call is not enough to compensate us for the greater risk we're taking on.

As such, picking a put strike price level for that is out of the money for WMT will not work in our favor and we'll be limiting our profits. However, this is the case with WMT because the outlook is bearish right now. Thus, the call premiums are low because no one is particularly interested in buying calls on a falling stock.

If conditions were bullish enough, you would see higher call premiums which would enable you to take a larger risk. Remember that your strike price levels need to match up with the S/R levels on the chart and that reward-risk ratio alone should not govern these levels.

With WMT, if the 100 level was beyond a strong support zone, where the price was unlikely to hit and 130 just before a resistance zone, this makes the trade more likely to hit its maximum profit potential than the prior case which gave us a higher reward risk. So always remember to correlate your levels to what you see on the chart.

If the stock price does decrease, you have a decision to make. You can either exercise your put, take that profit and have it offset your long position loss by closing that leg out as well, or you can keep your long position going and simply move the collar down by picking lower strike prices for your put and call.

This does increase the cost of your trade but if you're quite certain of the bullish nature of the market, this might be a good option to pursue. Having said that, I do not recommend beginners practice this because it is easy to fall into the trap of adding to a losing trade and trying to earn back the money you lost in the previous position. Thus, leave adjustments to when you have built up more skills.

The best method of making collars work for you is to purchase LEAPS. LEAPS are simply longer-term options with expiry date which are a year or even two years out in advance. This way, you can be certain that your trade will hit its maximum reward level, no matter what. Just remember to risk the correct amount on the trade.

Collars should form the basis of your trading operations and it's a good idea to have a few collars going simultaneously in a few different instruments. This way, you'll consistently have profits flowing in and you can use these profits as a bedrock from which you can trade directionally.

Directional trading will bring you bigger profits but carry higher risk and require greater mental skills to execute and wring every last cent of profit out of them. As we've seen with the two options strategies thus far, risk pretty much takes care of itself and all you have to do is to maintain the trade every once in a while, especially near the expiry dates.

Richard Bloom

The next strategy we'll be looking at is the "Spread Trade".

Chapter 7: Vertical Call Spreads

Call spreads require less upfront capital than the previous strategies we've looked at--the collar and the covered call. While the covered call is a steady income earner for the main long position and the collar works with speculative and investment positions, call spreads are purely speculative.

The vertical in the name refers to the way the trade is structured and how it presents itself when viewed as part of the option chain. Options spread trades are a slightly more advanced form of trading and prior to getting into these strategies, it is best if you gain a thorough understanding of the collar and make steady income with it.

Bull Call Spread

The bull call spread enables you to make money in up-trending markets. The beauty of this strategy is that you can adjust your spread on the basis of the level of market bullishness, with more bullish markets requiring a high speed and mildly bullish ones requiring a lower spread.

The trade consists of two legs, a long call and a short call with the same expiration month. The long call should be close to or at the money and is the primary instrument for profit in this strategy. The short call should be decided on the same principles as the short on the covered call, with a strike price just far enough to provide a good premium but not too close that the market price would breach it.

As you can imagine the strike price levels depend heavily on the level of bullishness of the market. Generally speaking, it is a good idea to place your short call just beyond a strong resistance level. Let's look at how the numbers work via an example.

Profit and Loss Numbers

Walmart, WMT, is currently trading at $110.62. Let's assume a bullish outlook for the stock but not a heavily bullish one. Assuming we set an exit time of a month for this trade to work out within, the August 110 call, which is technically at the money, will cost us $2.44 to purchase. Alternatively, you could also purchase the 112 call which can be made for $1.41. Let's go with the latter since this reduces our cost basis.

For the short call, given that our outlook is only for a month, a strike price of 120 seems reasonable since to hit this level, a gain of 9% is necessary which seems unlikely to happen in just a month. The premium we receive for this option is $0.04. Thus, our numbers are:

Cost of trade entry= Premium paid for 112 call - premium received for 120 call = 1.41-.04= $1.37.

This also happens to be our maximum risk on this trade. If the market price of the stock decreases, the long call will expire worthlessly but the short call premium will remain the same and thus cap our risk.

Maximum reward= Strike price of short call - Strike price of long call - Premium paid for long call + Premium received for short call = 120-112-1.41+0.04= $6.63

This gives us a very tidy 4.43 reward to risk ratio which any directional trader would give an arm and a leg for. You can increase the profit potential by laying around with the long call strike price but remember that your short call strike has to be taken into account as well.

Furthermore, you will also need to place your strike prices at sensible levels with respect to S/R zones. Your short call should ideally be beyond a strong resistance level or if your outlook is a month or less, beyond some level which is sure to give pause to price and delay its advance past it. The best level for a short call would be right at the resistance level since any price beyond this will result in an opportunity loss and any level below this will result in a less than maximum reward.

What if the market turns out to behave in the exact opposite manner than what you predicted? Well, in that case, you will need to adjust your trade by either moving your spread to lower levels, that is, picking lower strike prices for both legs and switching to a bear call spread strategy which we'll look at in the next section.

All in all, the bull call spread relies on your reading market conditions correctly and more importantly, picking the right strike prices in line with S/R zones. If you happen to see price in a range, then using the bottom boundary as the long strike price and the top boundary as the short strike price is an excellent method to make money every month.

Start by implementing this in ranges and then progress to slow-moving trends. Only once you've mastered these should you move onto fast trends.

Bear Call Spread

The bear call spread is designed to take advantage of bearish market situations. Now, keep in mind that in addition to bearish overall conditions, you can also make use of this strategy in ranging conditions, such as at the top of the range.

If you find a price at or near the top boundary of a range then implementing this strategy with a shorter-term expectation for it to work will bring you good profits in the short run. The key as always is to ensure that your risk is covered and that your strike prices are in line with S/R environment.

The bear call, just like the bull call, has two legs to it. There is a short call and a long call but in the bear call spread's case, the short call is below the long call. The higher strike price long call caps our maximum risk while the short leg functions as the primary profit generator.

The short call should be at the money or as close to it as possible with the long call just beyond a strong S/R level. Let's look at an example of how the numbers work for this strategy.

Profit and Loss Numbers

Sticking with good old WMT, we have a market price of $110.62 as of the previous close. Let's assume this is at the top of a range currently and we expect the range to hold. Mind you, we don't know for sure which is why every trade needs risk mitigation.

Your first step is to buy a call with a strike price beyond the resistance level. This will give you premium income and obviously, the closer it is to the market price, the more income you will earn. Of course, the danger of having it too close is that a momentary spike might jeopardize your strategy so you need to balance it out.

Let's say that 115 is a good level and that we expect this to hold for at least a month. The August 115 call costs us $0.50 to buy.

Next, we sell a call which is as close to the money as possible. As with the bull call spread, let's pick the 112 level which will provide us with $1.32 in premium income. As a side note: the prices I've quoted for the 112 strike price option are different because remember that when you buy, you pay the ask price and when you sell, you pay the bid. In this case, $1.32 is the bid price.

Our numbers work out as:

Maximum gain/cost of trade entry= Premium from short call - Premium from long call

= 1.32-0.4= $0.92

Maximum loss= Strike price of long call - Strike price of short call - cost of trade entry = 115-112-0.92=$2.08

As you can see, this trade has a reward-risk ratio of just 0.44. However, this is still a profitable strategy due to the fact that the win rate is usually quite high with this strategy. Recall the win rate and average win calculations we performed in the chapter on risk and you can figure out what win rate is required to break even and profit on this strategy.

Even this strategy can be adjusted to higher spread levels should you choose, but this should be done only if the S/R and the market environment supports readjustment. If you misread a bear trend and the market starts becoming bullish, adjustment is not going to do anything for you.

Both the spread trades require you to read market conditions thoroughly and this is why I recommend starting out with covered calls and collars which are market-neutral. Despite the lower risk levels of the vertical spread trades, you will have to incur a higher level of directionality with them and this exposes you to further risk.

The bear call spread is a good example of this. Given the high win rate it needs to make you money, it is far less forgiving of mistakes than other strategies. Thus, you need to have a very high level of market and order flow deciphering skills, coupled with the right mindset.

There is money to be made but you need to build the correct foundation before progressing forward.

Chapter 8: Challenges with Option Trade

Because of the listed four constraints, it becomes very imperative to be acquainted with and the listed acceptable profit-taking methods:

1. In distinction to stocks which can be managed for an infinite time, options have an ending. Trade length is restricted and once missed, an opportunity may not return all over again throughout the short lifetime of the option.

2. Long ways like "averaging down" (i.e., continual patronage on dips) don't appear to be acceptable for a decision making it is restricted.

3. Margin requirements can severely impact mercantilism capital necessities.

4. Multiple factors for option-value determination build it powerful to bank on an honest worthy move. As an example, the underlying stock moves favorably to change high profits on an option position, but various factors, like volatility, time decay, or dividend payment, could erode those gains inside.

This part of the book will discuss several very important

methodologies for some way and once to book profit in options trading.

Trailing Stop

A very well-liked profit taking strategy, equally applicable to option trading, is that trailing stop strategy whereby a pre-determined share level (say 5%) is prepared for a specific target. As an example, assume you get 10 option contracts at $80 (totaling $100) with $100 as profit target and $70 as a stop-loss. If you have attained $100, the trailing focus will be adding up to $95 (5% lower). Suppose that uptrend procedure with the amount moving to $120, the new trailing impeded and becomes $114, a further uptrend to $150 altering the trailing stop to $142.5. Now, if the price turns around and starts declining from $150, the options are excessively subscribed off at $142.5.

Trailing stop loss permits you to be aware and also from continuing protection against increasing gains and to shut the trade once the direction changes.

Traders use it in multiple variants, relying upon their strategy and furniture.

• As price appreciates, the proportion level is varied (initial 5% at $100 target is often changed to 5% or 7% at $120, per the trader's strategy).

• The initial stop-loss level is set at the same 5% level (instead of separately set $70).

- It can also be supported by underlying price movements, instead of the selection prices.

The key purpose is that the stop loss level has to be compelled to be set at neither small (to avoid frequent triggers) nor giant (making it unachievable).

Partial Profit Booking at Targets

Experienced traders typically follow a proven observation to book partial profits once the focus means is reached, say squaring off a 35% or 55% position if the first set target ($100) is achieved. It offers a pair of edges for decisions trading:

1. Partial profit booking shields the mercantilism capital to a far better extent, preventing money losses simply if there is a sudden price change, that's typically discovered in decisions option. Inside the said example, the businessperson can sell five contracts immediately (60%) once the set point of a target of $100 is attained. It permits him to retain $500 capital (out of the initial capital of $800 to buy for 10 contracts at $80).

2. A rest open position permits the businessperson to reap the promising future benefit. A focus hit of $120 offers a receipt of $720 ($120 x 6 contracts), resulting in a total of $1,100. Another productive means is to sell 60% or 70% of remaining, allowing an area for the added benefit at a consecutive rank. Let's assume three contracts are to close at $125 ($350 receipt) and also it is left paired and closed

at the price of $150 ($350 receipt), the total sale values are progressing to be $1,160 ($500 + $350 + $300).

Partial Profit Booking for Customers

Similar to what we've simply mentioned scenario, partial profits are engaged by traders at regular time intervals supported the remaining time to finish, if the position is in profit. Options are decaying assets. A significant portion of a option premium consists of additional decay worth (with intrinsic price accounting for the rest). Most veteran option keepers keep a detailed eye on decaying price and regularly verify positions and options moves towards finishing point to avoid extra loss of incessant time decay value whereas the position is the profit.

Buyers of a option position ought to bear in mind of incessant time decay effects and can shut the positions as a stop-loss live if coming back into the last month of finish with no clarity on a giant modification in valuations. Time decay can erode countless money, although the underlying price moves well.

Profit Booking Temporal Property for Sellers

The time decay of decisions naturally erodes their valuation as time passes, with the last month to termination seeing the fastest rate of abrasion. Option sellers profit by getting higher premiums at the start thanks to time decay worth, but it comes at the value of options trade who pay that prime premium at the start that they still lose throughout the time they hold the position. For sellers of short call or short place, the profit potential is restricted (capped to the premium received). Having pre-determined benefit levels (traders' set level like 40%/60%/80%) it is important to achieve, as margin value is at stake for option sellers. Inside the case of reversals, the restricted profit potential can quickly turn into a huge loss with the increasing requirements of more margin money.

Profit Booking on Fundamentals

Option commerce does not happen entirely on technical indicators. Many traders jointly take long positions as supported fundamentals analysis; therefore on learning from an occasional commerce capital demand.

For example, assume you have got a negative outlook; a few of stock leading to an extended place position with a couple of years to finish and so the target is achieved in nine months. Options trade cross-check the fundamentals once more, and if it is still favorable to the current status, the trade is the management onto (after discounting the time decay impact for long positions). If unfavorable factors (such as time decay or volatility) are showing adverse impacts, the profits have to be compelled to be engaged (or losses ought to be cut)

Option sellers profit by getting higher premiums at the start thanks to time decay worth, but it comes at the value of options trade who pay that prime premium at the start that they still lose throughout the time they hold the position. For sellers of short call or short place, the profit potential is restricted (capped to the premium received).

Averaging Up

Averaging down is one of the worst ways to follow inside the case of losses in options trading. Though it ought to be very appealing, it has to be compelled to be avoided. Instead, it's higher to shut the current chance position at a loss and start recently with a replacement one with an extended time to finish it. Remember, decisions have ending dates. Then after the date, they're trashy. Averaging down might suit stocks which can be command forever, but not decisions. Instead, averaging up might even be a good strategy to adopt for profit-making, provided there's sufficient time to finish and an honest outlook to the position.

For instance, if the target of $100 is secured, get another four contracts to boot to the amount bought earlier at $80. The common price is presently $((10*80 + 5*100)/15 = \$86.67)$. If the consecutive target of $120 is hit, get another three contracts, taking the common price to $92.22 for a whole of eighteen contracts. If the consecutive target of $150 is hit, sell all eighteen with a profit of $(150-92.22)*18 = \$1040$. Different variants embody additional shopping (say three additional at $150) and keeping a trailing loss (5% or $142.5).

All-Time Low Line

Options trading could also be an extraordinarily volatile game. No surprise, countries like China are taking their time to open up the market of their option. The extraordinarily volatile options market will offer the monumental probability to profit from it, but attempting to have interaction during this whereas not having decent knowledge, clearly determined profit targets, and stop-loss methodologies may result in failures and losses. Traders must be able to live up to the task by taking a glance at their ways on historical info and enter the options commerce world with real money with pre-decided ways to stop losses and ensure profit-taking.

Chapter 9: Options Trading Strategies

Options are conditional spinoff contracts that enable patrons of the contracts (option holders) purchase or sell a security at a selected worth. Option patrons are charged an amount known as "premium" by the sellers for the right. Could the market costs be unfavorable for option holders, they'll let the option expire worthlessly, so making certain the losses aren't over the premium. In distinction, option sellers (option writers) assume a bigger risk than the option consumers that is why they demand this premium.

Options are divided into "call" and "put" options. With a decision option, the client of the contract purchases the right to purchase the underlying asset within the future at a preset worth, known as exercise value or strike price. With a put option, the client acquires the right to sell the underlying quality within the future at the present worth.

Why Trade options instead of an instantaneous Asset?

There are some blessings to trading options. The Chicago Board of Option Exchange (CBOE) is that the largest such exchange within the world, giving options on a good sort of single stocks, ETFs and indexes. Traders will construct option methods starting from shopping for or selling one option to very advanced ones that involve multiple concurrent option positions.

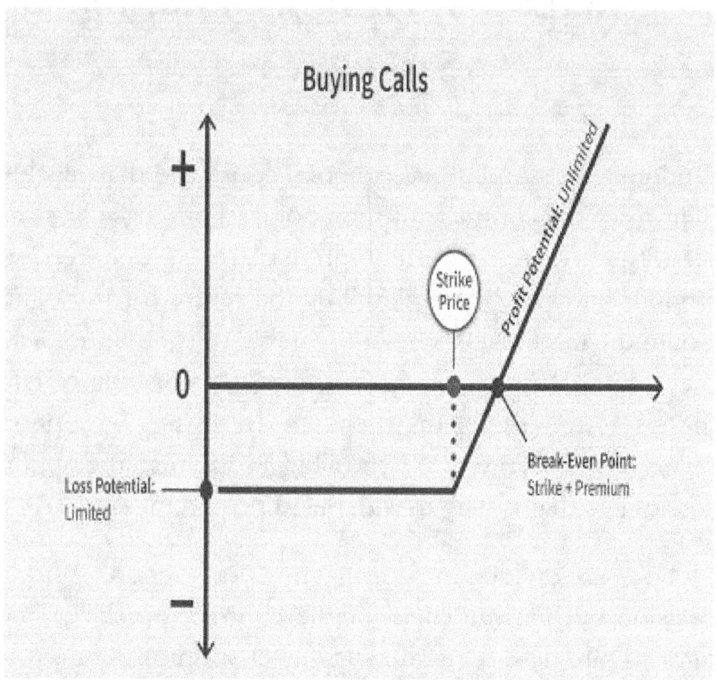

The following are basic option methods for beginners

Buying Calls (Long Call)

This is the popular strategy for traders who:

• are "bullish" or confident on selected stock, ETF or index and wish to limit the risk

Options Trading

- need to utilize leverage to require advantage of inflation

Options are leveraged instruments, i.e., they permit traders to amplify the profit by risking smaller amounts than would somewhat be needed if trading the underlying asset itself. A regular options contract on a stock controls a hundred shares of the underlying security.

Suppose a dealer needs to take a position $5,000 in Apple (AAPL), trading around $165 per share. With this quantity, he or she will purchase thirty shares for $4,950. Suppose then that the worth of the stock will increase by 10% to $181.50 over succeeding month. Ignoring any brokerage, commission or dealings fees, and the trader's portfolio can rise to $5,445, leaving the merchant with a net dollar come back of $495, or 10% on the capital invested with.

Now, let's say a decision option on the stock with a strike worth $165 that expires a couple of months from currently prices $5.50 per share or $550 per contract. Given the trader's offered investment budget, he or she will obtain 9 options for a price of $4,950. As a result of the option, the contract controls a hundred shares, the bargainers are effectively creating a deal on 900 shares. If the stock worth will increase 10% to $181.50 at expiration, the option can expire within the cash and be value $16.50 per share ($181.50-$165 strikes), or $14,850 on 900 shares. That's a net dollar come back of $9,990, or 200% on the capital invested with, a far larger come back compared to trading the underlying quality directly.

The trader's potential loss from a protracted decision is proscribed to the premium paid. Potential profit is unlimited, as the option payoff can increase at the side of the underlying quality worth till expiration, and there's theoretically no limit to however high it will go.

Buying Puts (Long Put)

This is the popular strategy for traders who:

• are pessimistic on selected stock, ETF or index, but need to require on less risk than with a short-selling strategy

• need to utilize leverage to take advantage of falling costs

A put option works the precise opposite method a decision option works, with the put option gaining worth because of the worth of the underlying decreases. While short-selling additionally permits a trader to exploit falling costs, the danger with a brief position is unlimited, as theirs, in theory, no limit on how high worth will rise. With a place option, if the underlying rises past the option's strike worth, the option can merely expire worthlessly.

Risk/Reward: Potential loss is proscribed to the premium bought the options. The utmost exploit the position is capped since the underlying worth cannot drop below zero, however, like an extended call option, the put option leverages the trader's come back.

Options Trading

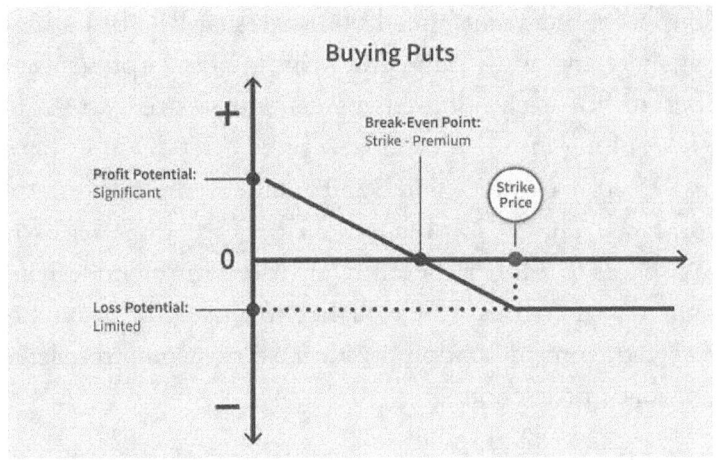

Covered Call

This is the popular position for traders who:

• Expect no amendment or a small increase within the underlying's worth

• Are willing to limit upper side potential in exchange for a few drawback protection

A preventive options strategy involves shopping for a hundred shares of the underlying quality and selling a call option against those shares. Once the bargainer sells the option, he or she collects the option's premium, so lowering the price basis on the shares and providing some drawback protection. In return, by selling the option, the bargainer is agreeing to sell shares of the underlying at the option's strike worth, thereby capping the trader's upper side potential.

Suppose a merchant buys 1,000 shares of BP (BP) at $44 per share and at the same time writes ten call options (one contract for each hundred shares) with a strike worth of $46 expiring in one month, at a price of $0.25 in a share, or $25 in a contract and $250 total for the sum of the contracts. The $0.25 premium reduces the price basis on the shares to $43.75; therefore any drop in the underlying right down to this time will be offset by the premium received from the option position, so providing restricted drawback protection.

If the share worth rises on top of $46 before expiration, the short decision option is going to be exercised (or "called away"), which means the bargainers will need to deliver the stock at the option's strike worth. During this case, the bargainers can build a profit of $2.25 per share ($46 strike worth - $43.75 value basis).

However, this instance implies the bargainer doesn't expect BP to maneuver higher than $46 or considerably below $44 over the consequent month. As long as the shares don't rise higher than $46 and get referred to as a way before the options expire, the dealer can keep the premium free and clear and might continue marketing calls against the shares if he or she chooses.

Risk/Reward: If the share worth rises on top of the strike price before expiration, the short decision option is exercised and also the bargainer can deliver shares of the underlying at the option's strike value, even though it's below the value. In exchange for this risk, a preventive call strategy provides restricted drawback protection within the variety of premium received once merchandising the decision option.

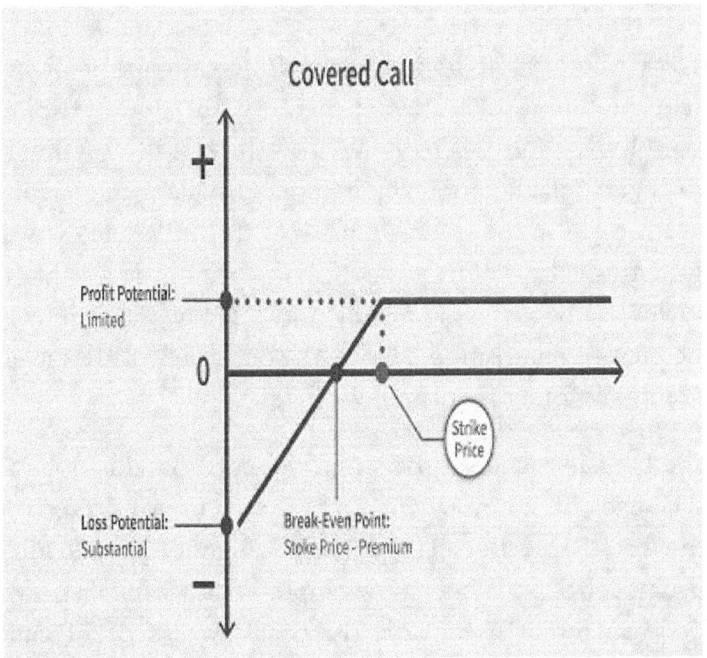

Protective Place

This is the popular strategy for traders who:

•Own the underlying quality and need to draw back protection.

A protecting place may be a long put, just like the strategy we mentioned above; but the goal, as the name implies, is drawn back protection versus making an attempt to exploit a downside move. If a bargainer owns shares that he or she is optimistic about within the long-term but needs to guard against a decline in the short run, they'll purchase a protecting place.

If the value of the underlying will increase and is higher than the put's strike price at maturity, the option expires worthlessly and also the trader loses the premium; however, still the good thing about the raised underlying worth has. On the opposite hand, if the underlying worth decreases, the trader's portfolio position loses price; however, this loss is essentially prevented by the gain from the put option position. Hence, the position will effectively be thought of as an insurance strategy.

The bargainer will set the strike worth below this price to scale back premium payment at the expense of decreasing drawback protection. This may be thought of as deductible insurance. Suppose, as an example, that a capitalist buys 1,000 shares of Coca-Cola (KO) at a worth of $44 and needs to guard the investment against adverse price movements over the subsequent 2 months. The subsequent put options are available:

Options Trading

This month options Premium

$44 put	$1.23
$42 put	$0.47
$40 put	$0.20

The table shows that the price of protection will increase with the amount thereof. For instance, if the bargainers need to guard the investment against any call worth, he or she will obtain ten at-the-money put options at a huge price of $44 for $1.23 in a given share, or $123 in a contract, for a total value of $1,230. However, if the bargainers are willing to tolerate some level of drawback risk, he or she will opt for less expensive out-of-the-money options like a $40 put. During this case, the price of the option position is going to be considerably lower at solely $200.

Risk/Reward: If the value of the underlying stays

constant or rises, the potential loss is going to be restricted to the option premium, that is paid as insurance. If, for an instant, the worth of the underlying decreases suddenly, the loss in the capital is going to be offset. It will rise within the option's worth and is proscribed to the distinction between the initial stock price and strike price and the premium that acquired the option. Within the example above, at the strike worth $40, the loss is proscribed to $4.20 per share ($44 - $40 + $0.20).

Other Options Methods: These methods could also be a bit additional advanced than merely buying calls or put;, however, they're designed to assist you better manage the danger of options trading:

• Coated Options Strategy Or Buy-Write Strategy: Stocks are bought, and also the capitalist sells options on the constant stock. The number of shares you obtain ought to be the image of the number of options contracts you oversubscribed.

• Married Place Strategy: when shopping for a stock, the capitalist buys put options for the same variety of shares. At constant time, you'll sell the same variety of call options at a better strike worth.

• Protecting Collar Strategy: a capitalist buys an option that does not require money, whereas at an equivalent time writing which does not require money call option for the same stock.

Options Trading

- Long Straddle Strategy: The capitalist buys a call option and a put option at an equivalent time. Each option ought to have a similar strike value and expiration date.

- Long Strangle Strategy: The capitalist buys an out-of-the-money decision option and a place option at constant time. They need constant expiration date; however, they have totally different strike costs. The put strike worth ought to be below the option strike price.

The Bottom Line: Options provide various methods for investors to exploit trading underlying securities. There's a spread of ways involving totally different combinations of options, underlying assets, and different derivatives. Basic ways for beginners embrace buying calls, buying puts, marketing protective calls, and shopping for protecting puts. There are benefits to trading options instead of underlying assets, like drawback protection and leveraged returns; however, there are disadvantages just like the demand for direct premium payment.

Chapter 10: Profit Drivers

Profit drivers contribute to various means that have a noticeable impact on the bottom line of your business. Commerce accounts and profit and loss statements generally contain data on profit drivers for a particular business and can be extracted very minutely. By the distinctive profit drivers in your business and specializing in them, you'll attain the foremost effective growth results.

Profit drivers are classified as financial and non-financial.

Financial Profit Drivers

Financial profit drivers are directly associated with buck figures and are most typically thought-about regarding profit. Examples include:

• Price

• Fixed costs

• Variable costs

• Sales volume

• Worth of debt

- Inventory.

A financial profit driver relation might even be expressed as a:

- Selection (e.g. average style of sales per month)

- Buck figure (e.g. the common sale per client)

- Share (e.g. share of purchasers)

The criteria for the calculation of financial profit drivers are normally clearly reflected in your money statements.

Non-Financial Profit Drivers

Non-financial profit drivers additionally impact the bottom line, even supposing they're not expressed in dollar terms. Client satisfaction, for instance, can continually impact on the number of products sold-out and increase or decrease profit. Weather conditions might also impact sales.

Non-financial profit drivers include:

- Productivity

- Shopper satisfaction

- Quality of the product or service

- Coaching of workers

- Worker satisfaction (morale)

- Business culture and values
- Product and method of innovation
- Market share
- Worker safety.

Ranking Your Profit Drivers

Think about your own business and therefore the relative importance of its profit drives. Once you have got to determine your profit drivers, compute why they're necessary for the success of a business. This can assist you to rank your profit drivers from most vital to the smallest benefit in relation to their direct impact on our business goals.

The top profit drivers common to most businesses include:

- increasing sales (turnover)
- reducing the price of sales
- reducing overhead expenses.

Calculating Your Business's Turnover

One of the foremost vital profit drivers is sales revenue or turnover. Three easy factors verify turnover for a business:

- Range of consumers
- The average range of transactions per client annually

- The average worth of dealing

Use the subsequent interactive calculator to assist you in computing the turnover. Once you have got a scan and understood the instance, you'll be able to know or look for the numbers that are relevant to your business also into the calculation to ascertain your turnover.

To improve your business's turnover, you would like to enhance its performance in one or additional of those three areas. You want to acquire additional customers or sell to them more usually or increase the quantity you sell to every one of them.

Turnover

Use this formula to calculate your turnover.

Turnover = number of client x average number of dealing per customer x average worth of every transaction.

Number of consumers (e.g. 100)

The average range of transactions per client (e.g. 10)

The average worth of every dealing (e.g. $100)

Setting a Profit Goal

Your profit goal is that the quantity of the cash you would like to have to fulfill a variety of present commitments that are necessary to you and the long run of your business.

Figuring out a profit goal can assist you to direct your actions and methods (once you've known your profit drivers) to achieve your target.

To set a profit goal, you'll get to take into account the following:

- Prices (both fastened and variable)
- Owner's annual financial gain
- Operative expenses (fixed and variable)
- Come on borrowed capital
- Come for risk
- Come for future growth.

We advocate that you operate together with your business authority to set a level of degree of acceptable profit goal for your business.

Fixed (overhead) prices

Your fastened prices (also known as overhead costs) are indirect value measures in cost that promise to hold a related amount despite your production outcome - this includes things like house and bill payment, and maintaining prices for your work facility, licensing fees, insurance, and accounting.

Variable prices

Your direct prices, like labor and value of raw materials, are solely incurred once you're making or producing a product, though they're not counted as fastened prices.

Owner's Annual Financial Gain or Income

When estimating your financial gain, you ought to use a quantity you pay workers who do the work you're doing. It ought to embody superannuation, however, it shouldn't be an inflated pay.

Return of Starting Capital

Return of initial starting capital is known as adequate return of capital you have initially invested with, a minimum that equates to long run bank interest, also as an extra come back based on the extent of risk.

Return for Risk

This is the comeback you expect, leaving the related risks - running a business has additional risk than saving funds in a bank.

The return for risk ought to be calculated in direct proportion to the risks concerned. For instance, if you endowed in an exceedingly very speculative business venture with the rare chance of success, you'd expect a high rate of coming back if it did prove booming.

Return for Future Growth

This is the quantity you would like to invest for future growth and development of your business. You'll have to be compelled to expand your premises once a couple of years, develop an innovative means give a service or new product, or develop a brand new marketing strategy.

Chapter 11: Option Greek Four Factors to Measure Risks

An option's price is influenced by a variety of things that may either facilitate or hurt trader's reckoning on the kind of positions they have to take. Productive traders perceive the factors that influence options evaluation, that embody the Greeks—are the means of calculating measure that shows how obvious an option is to the specific duration, tacit volatility, and evaluation changes in an underlying security.

The four basic Greek risk measures of trading options are **delta, theta, vega**, and **gamma**.

Key Takeaways

• Delta could be alive of the modification in an option's worth or premium ensuing from a change within the underlying asset.

• Gamma measures Delta's rate of amendment over time still because of the rate of change within the underlying asset. Gamma helps forecast value moves within the underlying asset.

- Theta measures the speed of the duration decay at the value of the option premium.

- Vega measures the chance of changes in tacit volatility or the progressive expected volatility of the underlying asset value.

Understanding Option Contracts

Options contract is majorly to render help for a portfolio. The goal is to set an offset potential for any unwanted to different investments. Options contracts are used in speculating on whether or not an asset's value may rise or fall.

In short, a decision option offers the holder of the option the proper right to shop for the underlying plus whereas a place option permits the holder to sell the underlying asset. An option is exercised, which means they will be reborn to shares of the underlying plus at a nominal value known as the strike price. Each option has an ending date known as an expiration date and a value related to it called the premium.

The premium or value of an option is sometimes supported by an option evaluation model, like Black-Sholes, that results in fluctuations in value. Greeks are sometimes viewed in conjunction with an option value model to assist you to have adequate knowledge and gauge associated risks.

How much an option's premium, or market price, fluctuate leading up to its expiration is termed volatility. Value fluctuations are caused by the range of things together with the money conditions of the corporate, economic conditions, geopolitical risks, and moves within the whole markets.

The implied volatility symbolizes the market's situation of the chances that an asset's value can be altered. Investors use tacit volatility, known as tacit vol., to forecast or anticipate future moves within the security or stock and in the option's worth. If volatility is anticipated to extend, which means tacit vol. is rising, the premium for an option can increase still.

Influences on an Option's Value

Table one below lists the main influences on each decision and place the option's value. The plus or minus signs show the option's value direction ensuing from a modification in one in every of the listed variables.

For example, once there's an increase in tacit volatility, there's a rise within the value of an option as long as alternative variables stay static.

Decrease to Expiration Increase within the Underlying Decrease in the Underlying

Options	Rise in Volatility	Reduction in Volatility	Rise in Time to Expiration	Reduction in Time to Expiration	A rise in the Underlying	Reduction in the Underlying
Calls	+	-	+	-	+	-
Puts	+	-	+	-	-	+

Table 1: Major influences on an option's value

Bear in mind that results can dissent counting on whether or not a trader is long or short. If a trader is long on a decision option, an increase in tacit volatility is favorable as a result of higher volatility is often priced into the option premium. On the opposite hand, if a trader has established a brief decision option position, an increase in tacit volatility can have an inverse (or negative) impact; the author of a naked option, whether or not a place or a decision, wouldn't enjoy an increase in volatility as a result of writers need the worth of the option to say no. Writers are sellers of options. Once an author sells a call option, the author will not need the stock value to rise on top of the strike as a result of the vendor would exercise the option, if it does. In alternative words, if the stock's value rose high enough, the vendor would have to be compelled to sell shares to the option-holder at the strike price once the value was higher.

Sellers of options get paid a premium to assist complete the chance of getting their options exercised against them. Marketing options are additionally known as shorting.

Tables two and three show equivalent variables in terms of long and short decision options. The keynote is the decrease in tacit volatility reduced time to expiration, and a fall within the value of the underlying security can profit the short decision holder.

At an equivalent time, a rise in volatility, a larger time remaining on the option and an increase within the underlying can profit the long decision holder.

A short place holder secures gain from a decrease in tacit volatility, a reduced time remaining till expiration, and an increase within the value of the underlying security whereas a protracted place holder benefits from a rise in tacit volatility, a larger time remaining till expiration, and a decrease within the value of the underlying security.

Call Options

	Rise in Volatility	Reduction in Volatility	Rise in Time to Expiration	Reduction in Time to Expiration	A rise in the Underlying	Reduction in the Underlying	
Long	+	-	+	-	+		-
Short	-	+	-	+	-		+

Table 2: Major effect on both short and long call option's value

Rise in Volatility	Reduction in Volatility	Rise in Time to Expiration	Reduction in Time to Expiration	A rise in the Underlying	Reduction in the Underlying	
Long	+	-	+	-	-	+
Short	-	+	-	+	+	-

Table 3: Major influences on a brief and long place option's value

Interest rates give an impression of a negligible role in most of the positions throughout the lifetime of most option trades. Nevertheless, a lesser-known Greek, Rho, gives the value of the sign of changes in income rates on an option's worth. Typically, higher interest rates create decision options more expensive and place options more cost-effective, all different things being equal.

All of the aforementioned provide context for an examination of the risk classes accustom and gauge the relative impact of those variables.

Keep in mind; the Greeks facilitate traders to project changes in an option's value.

The Greeks

Vega	Theta	Delta	Gamma
Calculating the Impact of a Change in Volatility calculating Impact of a Change in Remaining time	Calculating the Impact of a Change in the Price of Underlying	Calculating the speed of Change of Delta	

Table 4 describes the four primary risk measures—the Greeks—that a business owner ought to contemplate before opening an option position.

Delta

Delta could be the evidence of the modification in degree option's value (that is, the premium of an option) ensuing from a modification within the underlying security. The worth of Delta ranges from -100 to zero for puts and zero to 100 for calls (is a multiple of 100 to alter the decimal number). Puts create negative delta as a result of it, they need a negative relationship with the underlying security; that's, place premiums fall once the underlying security rises and the other way around.

Additionally, call options tend to be a positive relationship within the worth of the underlying asset. If the underlying asset's value rises, so will the decision premium provided; there aren't any changes in different variables like tacit volatility or time remaining till expiration.

If the value of the underlying plus falls, the call premium will decline provided all factors stay constant.

A good method to visualize Delta is to consider a race track. The tires represent the Delta, and also the accelerator represents the underlying value. Low Delta options are like race cars with economy tires. They won't get a great deal of traction once you speedily accelerate. On the opposite hand, high Delta options are like drag racing tires. They supply heaps of traction once you tread on the gas, Delta values nearer to 1.0 or -1.0 offers the best levels of traction.

For example, suppose that one out-of-the-money option features a Delta of 0.25, and another in-the-money option features a Delta of 0.80. A $1.00 increase within the value of the underlying plus can cause a $0.25 increase within the initial option and a $0.80 increase within the second possibility. Traders searching for the best traction might want to think about high Deltas, though these options tend to be costlier in terms of their value basis since they're doubtless to expiry.

An at-the-money option, which means the option's strike value and also the underlying asset's price are equal, which is Delta worth of roughly fifty (0.5 while not the decimal shift). This means the premium can rise or fall to some extent with a one-point move up or down within the affected security.

For instance, if the out- money call option is Delta of 0.5 and wheat rises by ten cents, the premium on the option can increase by close to five cents (0.5 x ten = five) or $250 (each cent in a very premium is price $50).

Delta changes because the options become additionally profitable or in-the-money. In-the-money implies that a profit exists because of the option's strike value being additionally favorable to the underlying's price. In as much option gets more cash, Delta approaches one hundred on the call and -100 on a put, and there is an alteration from the price of the underlined worth.

In this effect, at Delta, the range worth of -100 and 100, the option shows that they are underlying security in terms of value changes. This behavior happens with very little or no duration as most of the worth of the option is intrinsic.

Probability of Being Profitable

Delta is often used during the decision, making the chance of an option being in-the-money at expiration. As an example, an out-of-the-money call option with a 0.20 Delta has roughly a 20% probability of being in-the-money at expiration, whereas a deep-in-the-money decision possible with a 0.95 Delta has roughly ninety-five % probability of being in-the-money at expiration.

The assumption is that the costs follow a log-normal distribution, sort of a coin flip.

On a high level, this implies that traders will use Delta to live the chance of a given possibility or strategy. Higher Deltas could also be appropriate for risky, high-reward methods with low win rates whereas lower Deltas could also be ideally fitted to low-risk strategies with high win rates.

The premium or value of an option is sometimes supported by an option evaluation model, like Black-Sholes, that results in fluctuations in value. Greeks are sometimes viewed in conjunction with an option value model to assist you to have adequate knowledge and gauge associated risks.

Delta and Directional Risk

Delta is often occasionally used while deciding on what the directional risks involve. The Positive Delta is long (buy) at the open assumptions, negative Delta is short (sell) open market assumptions; also neutral Delta is neutral at the market assumptions.

When you purchase a decision option, you might like a positive Delta since the worth can increase at the side of the underlying asset price. Once you purchase a put option, you wish a negative Delta wherever the value can decrease if the underlying asset price suddenly rises.

Three things to stay in mind with Delta:

1. Delta tends to extend nearer to expiration for close to or at-the-money options.

2. Delta is additionally evaluated by gamma that may be alive of Delta's rate of modification.

3. Delta may also amend in reaction to tacit volatility changes.

Gamma

Gamma calculates the steadiness of alteration in Delta over time. Since Delta values are perpetually ever-changing with the underlying asset's value, Gamma is employed to speed of modification and provide traders with a plan of what to expect within the future. Gamma values are highest for at-the-money options and lowest for those deep in- or out-of-the-money.

While Delta changes support the underlying asset value, Gamma may be a constant that represents the speed of the amendment of Delta. This makes Gamma helpful for determining the steadiness of Delta, which might be accustomed to verify the chance of an option reaching the strike value at expiration.

For example, suppose that 2 options have constant Delta worth; however, one possibility features a high Gamma and one has a low Gamma. The option with the higher

Gamma can have the next risk since an unfavorable move within the underlying asset will have an outsized impact. High Gamma values mean that the option tends to expertise volatile swings, which may be a dangerous factor for many traders searching for foreseeable opportunities.

A good beginning is to consider Gamma as is used to calculate readiness of an option's chance. If Delta represents the likelihood of being in-the-money at expiration, Gamma represents the steadiness of that change in the long-run.

An option which has an increased Gamma and a 0.76 Delta could have less of an opportunity of expiring in-the-money than an occasional Gamma option with an equivalent Delta.

Example of Gamma

Table five shows what proportion of Delta changes following a one-point move within the worth of the underlying. Once call options are deep out-of-the-money, they often have a little Delta as a result of changes within the underlying generate small changes in valuation. However, the Delta becomes larger because the decision possibility gets closer to the fund.

Table 5: has a variation in Delta in as much the point progress within the initial value that is underlying.

In Table 5, Delta is increasing as we try to read the number to right, and it's shown with values for Gamma at totally different levels of the underlying. The column showing profit or loss (P/L) of 200 which represents the money strike of 930, and every column represents a one-point change within the underlying.

At-the-money Gamma is -0.79, which implies that for each one-point move of the underlying, Delta can increase by precisely 0.79. (For each Delta and Gamma, the decimal has been shifted 2 digits by multiplying by one hundred.)

If you progress right to a successive column, that represents a one-point move higher to 931 from 930, you'll see that Delta is -53.13, a rise of .79 from -52.34.

Delta rises as this short decision possibility moves into the money, and also the negative sign means the position is losing as a result of it's a brief position. (In various words, the level of Delta is not positive.)

Therefore, with a negative Delta of -51.34, the position can lose 0.51 (rounded) points in premium with a successive one-point rise within the underlying.

There are some extra points to have in mind:

1. The smallest and deep-in-the-money options.

2. Gamma is best once the option gets close to the money.

3. It is positive in long-term options and negative for brief options.

Theta

Theta measures the speed in time decay within the value of an option premium.

Time decay symbolizes the decay of an option's worth or value because of the passage of the time. As time passes, the prospect of an option being profitable or in-the-money lessens. Time decay tends to accelerate because the expiration date of an option attracts closer as a result of there's less time left to earn a benefit from the trade.

Theta is usually negative for one option since time moves in the same direction. As shortly as an option is purchased by a marketer, the clock starts ticking, and also the worth of the option instantly begins to diminish till it expires, worthless at the predefined expiration date.

Theta is nice for sellers and dangerous for consumers. An honest method to visualize it is to imagine an hourglass within which one aspect is that the purchaser and also the alternate side is the marketer. The client should decide whether or not to exercise the option before time runs out. However, in the meantime, the worth is flowing from the buyer's facet to the seller's side of the sandglass. The movement might not be very fast, however, it's a nonstop loss, useful for the client.

Theta values are continually negative for long options and can always have zero duration at expiration since time solely moves in one direction, and time runs out as soon as an option expires.

Example of Theta

An option premium that has no intrinsic worth, or no profit, can decline at an increasing rate as expiration nears.

Table 6 shows theta values at totally different time intervals for an S&P five hundred Dec at-the-money call option. The strike value is 930.

As you'll see, Theta will increase because the expiration date gets nearer (T+20 is expiration). At T+18 or seven days before it expires, theta is now 94.3, so during this case tells it to tell us that the option is currently at a shortage of $93.30 per day, starting from $45.00 per day at T+1.0 once the theoretic merchandiser is opened.

Source: Fictitious knowledge, for illustration functions solely

Table 6: Theta values for brief S&P Dec 930 call option

Theta values seem sleek and linear over the long-run; however, the slopes become steeper for at-the-money options because the expiration date grows close to. The foreign value or duration of the in- and out-of-the-money options is extremely low close to expiration as a result of the chance of the value reaching the strike price is low.

In different words, there's a lower chance of earning a profit close to expiration as time runs out. At-the-money options could also be additional probably to succeed in these costs and earn a profit; however, if they don't, the ad extrinsic worth should be discounted over a brief amount.

Some further points about Theta to think about when trading:

1. Theta may be high for out-of-the-money options if they carry heaps of implied volatility.

2. Theta is usually highest at the money options since less time is required to earn a profit with a value move within the underlying.

3. Theta can increase sharply as time decay accelerates within a previous couple of weeks before expiration and may severely undermine a long option holder's position, particularly if tacit volatility declines at the equal time.

Vega

Vega measures the chance of changes in tacit volatility or the modern expected volatility of the underlying asset value. Whereas Delta measures actual value changes, Vega is targeted on changes in expectations for future volatility.

Higher volatility makes options costlier since there's a larger chance of meeting the strike value at some point.

Vega tells us roughly how much an option value can increase or decrease given rise or decrease within the level of tacit volatility. Option sellers enjoy a fall in silent volatility; however, it's simply the reverse for option consumers.

It's vital to recollect that silent volatility reflects value activities within the options market. Once option costs are bid up as a result of the additional consumers, tacit volatility can increase.

Long option traders take pleasure in valuation being bid up, and short option traders take pleasure in costs being bid down. This can be why long options have a positive Vega, and short options have a negative Vega.

Additional points to stay in mind relating to Vega:

1. Vega will increase or decrease and reflect the change in the price changes of the underlying asset, because of changes in silent volatility.

2. Vega will increase in reaction to speed moves within the underlying asset.

3. Vega falls because the option gets nearer to expiration.

Chapter 12: Steps to Extend Your Option Trading Profits

It is very imperative during trading to note the instrument which you can maximize to a level profit potential after you take your trade. You'll be able to increase your profits once trading options if you think about the two straightforward steps the book goes to stipulate below.

I want to ask you about an issue first:

Have you ever been stuck by sitting in front of the PC screen all weekend scanning through thousands of stocks trying to find the simplest people to trade within the subsequent week?

If your answer is affirmative, has your mind begun to marvel off to different stuff you would love to be doing together with your time?

If so, you have to be a part of the club!

You and the rest aren't different as you may be used to this during this very situation a few years in the past when someone was new. You started within the markets.

It will be simple to urge being sucked into this situation as there are several programs out there teaching the following approach:

- Grab a strategy and stir up your trading charts
- Scan through the total universe of stocks trying to find an explicit value pattern
- Make a note of the stock you're about to follow for the subsequent week

In my expertise, this will cause a variety of issues that you just really need to avoid.

Not solely do scanning thousands of stocks on an everyday basis take heaps of your time, it may also cause some common mistakes particularly during trading options.

Scanning for Patterns may be a Suckers' Play for Options Traders

In several cases, stock scans are run searching for sure value patterns on the charts. Whereas this will cause an invention of some sensible-looking charts, it doesn't make them a sensible product to trade when engaging options.

If you may be commercializing options then you have to concentrate on worth patterns.

One of the foremost unmarked areas of the market by traders is that the liquidity within the product they're trading. This is often very true with the current market atmosphere that you are seeing when volumes are less than actual historical levels.

Liquidity describes the degree to the extent an asset or security is often quickly bought or sold-out within the market even though it didn't affect the asset's value.

It doesn't matter whether the chart pattern appears nice, if there isn't volume (and open interest if commerce options) in those products, then you may realize it is very tough to urge in and out of trades quickly and at reasonable costs.

You might end up adjusting the value of your orders varied with times to gratify the urge. Whereas this doesn't seem to be an enormous deal to regulate the value of your order by several pennies, it will add up to an enormous variety over a full series of trades.

For example, if you engage in trading options and realize that over time you have got to regulate the value of your orders by $.05-$.10 on each trade to urge in and out, that may cause an enormous price at the end of the year. Let's say you place a hundred trades over one year and with every one of these trades, you use ten options contracts.

Adjusting Your Price Can Cost You

If you have got to regulate the value of your orders by $.05 on each trade in order to have stuffed due to the shortage of liquidity, you let go $5000 right there simply on trade costs; 5 cents doesn't seem to be an enormous deal on one trade, however, after you do the mathematics over dozens of trades, it is often an enormous loss in the long-run.

Even if you manipulate the numbers on the trade cited above and only take every trade with one contract, you're still losing out on $500 over the course on 100 trades if you can't get stuffed at smart costs.

Now, I notice that not to give up on $.05 on each trade taken throughout the year; however, you'll be able to do the mathematics here and see that it can add up over time quickly.

So, what is often done to remedy this situation?

Scan Solely a Couple of Stocks for Option Trades

Instead of scanning thousands of stocks on an everyday basis, you can proceed by doing the simple thing by slimming the universe of stocks right down to a manageable range, for example, the universe of stocks is 40-45 names outside of these names don't care what's happening in the rest of the different sides of the market.

This allows you to urge to grasp the names on the list very well and ensure that they're the liquid product. It additionally cuts back on the amount of research time that's needed to remain active within the markets. I don't need to pay hours each weekend researching which product will be trading the subsequent week.

I don't assume that any of us wish to have that burden weekly.

Since the names on our list don't often change, we can gain an extremely nice experience with our few watch-lists of products.

How to Return Up With a Stock Watch List

If you're searching for a decent place to begin to work, I have enclosed a link below to free options commerce e-book that we've got made that has our Hot List of stocks that you wish to trade on an everyday basis.

The key to making a watch-list of stocks is to create a certain means of employing a wide-ranging list of products. We would like a mixture of stocks and ETF's at the side of a mix of various sectors further. The additional diversification you have got on your list the higher your results likely to be in the future. We discuss more on this method in additional detail within the next chapter.

Ensure You're Trading Liquid Options for Higher Profits

How can we check to ascertain that the product we are trading is liquid enough, so that we can get in and out of trades quickly and at sensible prices?

Since you prefer to trade options, I look into the liquidity of the options not the shares of stock. Once watching the options on a selected stock or ETF, I prefer to examine sensible volume and open interest unfolds across multiple different strike costs.

Seeing smart volume on one strike worth isn't enough because it possibly indicates some huge institutional trades. Confirm that you're seeing the quantity and open interest unfold across multiple different strikes.

This is a product that you withdraw from trading.

The rule of thumb is

You usually need to examine open interest on the option you are trying to go into business of at the minimum of 50 x the number of contracts that you are looking to trade; therefore, if you are trying to trade ten contracts, you might wish to see the open interest of a minimum of five hundred contracts.

You might also wish to see the good daily volume on its contract also, but that's not as crucial as the volume will vary counting on the time of day you're putting your trade.

It might not appear to be an enormous deal if you're simply trading 1-5 contracts to focus most attention on the liquidity numbers of the options. You almost certainly won't have a troublesome time in several cases obtaining stuffed on those little trades.

However, your goal is to grow your trading account size over time; therefore, you'll be able to increase the scale of your trades.

With this being the case, it's crucial to determine sensible habits currently. Now, after you go from trading one contract on your trades to ten contracts, you are already being programmed to appear for the nice liquidity.

This is a lesson that the majority of traders ought to learn the arduous approach to know. The most worse is finding yourself in an edge and not having the ability to urge out while you fail to regulate your worth multiple times. As we have shown earlier, this could result in some pretty giant trade prices over time.

Chapter 13: Maximize Your Option Commerce Profits

As traders, we would like to maximize our returns; therefore, very little tweak that we can build to our trading that may increase our profit, in the long-run, is well definitely worth the effort. Establishing a watch-list of the product will take some work at first as you ought to analyze and you are required to understand those names.

However, since that list of a product doesn't change fairly often, you'll be able to begin obtaining a diary of trades that you simply will learn from. In the long-run, this may truly prevent time loss and result in higher results.

Take the time currently to target liquidity and it'll result in higher returns within the end of the day.

Options Trading Mistake 1: Shopping for Out-Of-The-Money (OTM) Call Options

Buying OTM calls outright is one of the toughest ways to create cash systematically in options trading. OTM's decision options are appealing to new options traders as a result of their low cost.

It feels like a decent place to start: obtain an inexpensive call option and see if you'll be able to decide a winner. Shopping for calls might feel safe; as a result of it, match the pattern you're accustomed to going the current equity trader: buying low and check out to sell high. However, if you limit yourself to only this strategy, you'll lose cash systematically.

Consider marketing an OTM call option on a stock that you simply already own as your initial strategy. This approach is thought of as a lined call strategy.

What's nice concerning covered calls as a method is that the risk doesn't return from commercializing the option once the option is roofed by a stock position? It additionally has the potential to earn your financial gain on stocks once you're optimistic and also you are willing to sell your stock if it goes up in worth. This strategy will give you the "feel" for a way OTM option contract costs modification as expiration approaches and also the stock value fluctuates.

The risk, however, owns the stock – which risk is often substantial. Though selling the call option doesn't turn out a capital risk, it will limit your face, thus making chance risk. You involve in risk when you are to sell the stock upon the assignment if the market rises and your call is in practice.

How to develop your options trading approach? Scrutinize our free section for beginners, experienced, and specialists.

Options Trading Mistake 2: Misunderstanding Leverage

Most beginners misuse the leverage the option contracts provide, not realizing what proportion risk they're taking. Often, they're drawn to purchasing short-run calls. Since this can be the case, therefore often, it's value asking: is that the outright shopping for calls a "speculative" or "conservative" strategy?

The Master Leverage. The general rule for starting option traders: if you always trade a hundred shares heaps then persist with one option to begin. If you usually trade three hundred share heaps – those perhaps three contracts. This can be a decent check quantity, to begin with. If you failed to have success in these ranges, you may not have success with the larger size trades.

Options Trading Mistake 3: Having No Exit Arrangement

You've most likely heard it 1,000,000 times before, during your trading options, similar to stocks, it's crucial to regulate your emotions. This doesn't mean swallowing your every worry in an exceedingly super-human approach. It's a lot easier than that: Have a concept figure and continue it.

You should have an exit setup period, even during the period when things are going in your approached way, select an upper side exit point, a downside exit purpose, and your timeframes for every exit well in advance.

What of this, assume you get out quickly and you ignore some upper side on the table?

This is a classic trader's worry. Here's the most effective counterargument: What if you create profit more systematically, scale down your incidence of losses, and sleep intensively at night?

Define your exit plan. Whether or not you're shopping for or marketing options, an exit arrangement must be mandatory. It helps you to determine the patterns of trading. It additionally keeps your worries more in restraint.

Determine an upper side exit plan and also the worst-case situation you're willing to tolerate on the drawback. If you reach your upper side goals, clear your position and take your profits. Don't get greedy. If you reach your drawback stop-loss, yet again, you must clear your position. Don't expose yourself to additional risk by gambling that the option worth may return.

The temptation to violate this recommendation can most likely be sturdy from time to time. Don't get laid. If you want to build your plan then be persistent with it. Far too many traders create a concept then, as shortly because the trade is placed, toss and decide to follow their emotions.

Options Trading Mistake 4: Not Being Receptive to New Methods

Most of the option traders normally prefer to obtain out-of-the-money options or never sell in-the-money options. These absolutes appear silly— before you discover yourself in an exceeding trade that's stirred against you.

All seasoned options traders are there. Facing this situation, you're typically tempted to interrupt every kind of privacy rules.

As a dealer, you've most likely heard the same justification for doubling up to catch up. As an example, if you liked the stock at eight after you bought it, you've got to like it at fifty. It may be tempting to opt for additional and lower the net price basis on the trade. Be wary, though: What is sensible for stocks may not fly within the options world. Doubling up as an option strategy sometimes just doesn't make sense.

Be hospitable learning new option trading methods. Remember, options are derivatives, which suggest their costs don't move identical or maybe have the same properties. Time decay, whether or not sensible or unhealthy for the position, perpetually must be factored into your plans.

Options Trading Mistake 5: Trading Illiquid Options

Liquidity is all concerned with how quickly a merchant should buy or sell one thing while not inflicting a major price movement. A liquid market is one with prepared, active patronizer and sellers continuously.

Here's a different way to accept it: Liquidity refers to the likelihood that succeeding trade is going to be executed at a value equal to the last one, ensure you're trading liquid options for higher profits

How can we check to ascertain that the product we are trading is liquid enough, so that we can get in and out of trades quickly and at sensible prices?

Since you prefer to trade options, I look into the liquidity of the options not the shares of stock. Once watching the options on a selected stock or ETF, I prefer to examine sensible volume and open interest unfolds across multiple different strike costs.

Seeing smart volume on one strike worth isn't enough because it possibly indicates some huge institutional trades. Confirm that you're seeing the quantity and open interest unfold across multiple different strikes.

Stock markets are additionally liquid than option markets for a straightforward reason. Stock traders are trading only on one stock whereas option traders might have dozens of options contracts to settle on from.

For example, stock traders can flock to at least one variety of let's simply say, IBM stock, however, options traders may have six completely different expirations and an overplus of strike costs to settle on from. Additional selections, by definition, means that the options market can most likely not be as liquid because of the exchange.

A large stock like IBM is typically not a liquidity drawback for stock or options traders. The matter creeps in with smaller stocks. Take for example the SGT, an (imaginary) environment-friendly energy company with more promise, may only have stock trades once every week by the only appointment.

If probably the stock is illiquid, the option available on SGT can probably be even additionally inactive. This may typically cause unfold between the bid and raise value for the options to urge unnaturally wide.

For instance, if the bid-seeking spread is $0.30 (bid=$1.80, ask=$2.00), and are able to have $2.00 contract, that's a total of 10% of the value paid to determine the position.

It's never a decent plan to determine your position at a 10% loss right off the bat, simply by selecting an illiquid option with a large bid-ask spread.

Trading illiquid options drive up the price of doing business, and option trading prices are already higher, on a share basis than stocks. Don't burden yourself.

If you're trading options, confirm the open interest is at least equated to forty times the amount of contacts you would like to trade.

For example, to trade a ten-lot, your acceptable liquidity ought to be 10 x forty, or open interest which is at least four hundred contracts. Open interest symbolizes the quantity of outstanding option contracts of a strike worth and the time of expiry date that is bought or sold-out to open a position. Any gap transactions increase open interest, whereas closing transactions decrease it. Open interest is calculated at the closing of every business day. Trade liquid options and save yourself extra value and stress. There are many liquid opportunities out there.

Looking for tools to assist you to explore opportunities, gain insight, or act whenever the mood strikes? Cross-check the intelligent tools on our trading platform.

Mistake in Options Trading 6: Experiencing a Delay in Short Options

This mistake will be stewed down to one piece of advice: continually be prepared and willing to shop for back short options early.

Far too common, traders can wait too long to shop back for the options they've sold-out. There are 1,000,000 reasons why for instance:

- You don't wish to pay the commission.

- You're sporting the contract can expire mercilessly.

- You're hoping to eke simply a touch additional profit out of the trade.

Know when to shop back for your short options. If the short option fails, the OTM and you will purchase it back to require the chance off the table fruitfully, do it. Don't be cheap.

For example, what if you sold-out a $1.00 option and its current value is 15? You can decide that you don't sell it at a 15-cent option, to begin with, as a result of this, it will not have the expected worthwhile. Similarly, you shouldn't assume it's worth it to squeeze the initial few cents out of this trade.

Here's a decent rule of thumb: if you'll keep 80% or more of your initial gain from the sale of the option, you ought to think about shopping for it back. Otherwise, it's a virtual certainty. Once every day, a brief possibility can bite you back as a result of you waited too long.

Options Trading Mistake 7: Failure to Issue out Upcoming Events

Not all events within the markets are predictable; however, there are 2 crucial events to stay track of during trading options: earnings and dividends dates for your underlying stock.

For example, if you've sold-out calls and there's a dividend approach, it will increase the chance you will be appointed early if the option is already in-the-money. This is often very true if the dividend is anticipated to be great. That's as a result of options homeowners don't have any rights to a dividend. To collect, the option bargainers should exercise the option and obtain the underlying stock.

Be sure to issue forthcoming events; for instance, you want to understand the ex-dividend date. Additionally by steer beyond marketing options contracts with unfinished dividends, unless you're willing to simply accept the next risk of assignment.

Trading throughout earnings season typically means that you'll encounter higher volatility with the underlying stock – and frequently pay an inflated worth for the option. If you're progressing to obtain an option throughout the earnings season, one different choice is to buy one option and sell another, making a ramification

Options Trading Mistake 8: Garment into Spreads

Most starting options traders try and "leg into" a spread by shopping for the options first and marketing the second option later. They're attempting to lower the price by a couple of pennies. It merely isn't worth the risk, for sure.

Options Trading

Sound familiar? Most old options traders are burned by this situation too, and learned the arduous manner eventually.

Don't "leg in" if you would like to trade a spread. Trade a spread as a single trade. Don't combat additional market risk as it is needless.

For example, you would possibly obtain a decision and so try and time the sale of another call, hoping to squeeze a touch higher worth out of the second leg. This is often a losing strategy if the market takes a downswing. Consequently, you won't be ready to realize your spread. You may be cursed for an extended decision and no strategy to impact.

If you're attending to do that strategy, don't obtain a spread and wait around, hoping that the market can move in your favor. You possibly suppose that you'll be ready to sell it later at a better worth. That's an impossible outcome.

Always, continually treat a spread as one trade. Don't try to alter the item of temporal arrangement. You would like to urge the trade before the market starts taking place.

Looking for tools to assist you to explore opportunities, gain insight, or act whenever the mood strikes? Explore the brilliant tools on various trading medium.

The options trading bad method that is not well known: failure to know what to engage in once initiated.

If you sell options, simply remind yourself sometimes that you just will be appointed early, before the expiration date. Uncountable new options traders never accept assignment as an opportunity till it happens to them. It will be jarring if you haven't factored in an assignment, particularly if you're running a multi-leg strategy like long or short spreads.

For example, what if you're running an extended decision spread and also the higher-strike short option is assigned? Starting traders might panic and exercise the lower-strike long option to deliver the stock. However, that's most likely not the simplest call. It's typically hitherto selling the long option on the open market; capture the remaining time premium besides the option's inherent worth and use the yield toward buying the stock. Then you'll deliver the stock to the option holder at the upper strike worth.

An early assignment is one of those emotional, usually irrational, market events. There's usually no rhyme or reason when it happens. It simply happens. Even once the marketplace is signaling that it's a less-than-brilliant maneuver.

Think through what you'd do once appointed well earlier than time. The most effective defense against early assignment is to issue it by thinking early. Otherwise, it will cause you to form defensive, in-the-moment.

It will facilitate and contemplate market science, for

instance, that is additionally wise to exercise early

Also Ask Yourself: do you need your money currently or at expiration? Typically, individuals can wish money can versus cash later, which means **puts method** are sometimes more liable to early exercise **than calls**.

When exercising a decision means that the buyer should be willing to pay money to shop for the stock, versus later within the game. Typically, it's attributing to attend and pay that money later. However, if a stock is rising, less accomplished traders would possibly pull the trigger early, failing to appreciate, they exploit your time premium on the table. That is to show that the early assignment will be unpredictable.

Options Trading Mistake 10: Ignoring Index Options for Neutral Trades

Individual stocks will be quite volatile. For example, if there's a major unforeseen occurrence in a different company, it may rock the stock for a couple of days. On the opposite hand, even serious turmoil in an exceedingly major company that's a part of the five hundred most likely would not cause that index to fluctuate pretty much.

What's the moral of the story?

Trading options that are in support indexes can protect you from the large moves that news things can produce for individual stocks. Think about neutral trades on huge indexes and you'll minimize the uncertain impact of market news.

Consider trading ways that might be profitable once the market stays still sort of a short spread. Index change might be less rapid.

Short spreads are historically constructed to be profitable, even once the underlying worth remains identical. Therefore, short decision spreads are thought-about "neutral to bearish" and short place spreads are "neutral to optimistic." This is often one key distinction between long spreads and short spreads.

Remember, spreads involve over one option trade, and so incur over one commission. Keeps this in mind once creating your trading options!

Looking for tools to assist you to explore opportunities, gain insight, or act whenever the mood strikes? Cross-check the intelligent tools on our trading platform.

Chapter 14: Psychological Brick Ways for Handling Losses

Psychologists have written extensively regarding defense mechanisms individuals use to eradicate things that are unpleasant or prejudicial from their perceived reality. A fateful investment may be a good example of one thing anyone would love to reverse or undo. Sadly, the clock cannot be turned back, and it's better to manage the method psychologically than to undertake to form up the losses through risky investments.

Dysfunctional Brick Ways

When long-faced with losses, many of us use dysfunctional brick ways. These include:

• Suppression: attempting to suppress the negative feelings related to a loss may be troublesome as they are available to haunt you again. Money issues and loss-induced distress will simply develop into matrimonial or career-related problems or stress. You may find yourself casting off your frustrations on your family, colleagues or friends.

• Projection: it's not uncommon for those facing a giant loss to undertake or charge it on somebody or one thing else instead of taking responsibility for his or her own poor choices or excessive risk-taking.

• Denial and Self-Delusion: These dysfunctional brick strategies lead individuals to clutch failing investments within the vain hope that "they can go up once more." If to procure a dud, it's nearly always best to eliminate it and place no matter cash is left into one thing safer. In short, cut your losses and pass on.

Sound Brick Ways

Assuming you have got no legitimate claim against the vendor for your losses, or cannot afford to travel this route, it's necessary to come back to terms with the case. One substantive means of coping is solely to learn from your errors on how to recoup the losses over time by financing well and providentially within the future. This is often not a fast fix or "sure issue," however, it is very sensible to undertake. If you took excessive risks by trusting the wrong individuals or were just simply unlucky, you'll need a lot of carefulness along with diversifying your portfolio more within the future. Even though it takes years, you will well realize that you just get some or all of it back, and it's comforting to assume this would possibly happen.

Keep in mind that some investments merely do fail. There are incompetent, unethical and dishonest individuals within the business and anyone may be a victim; that's life and what doesn't kill you, will indirectly make you stronger.

Rationalization is beneficial and providing it is realistic. It's necessary to have knowledge of what your fellow did and why, for example, were you tempted by the lure of massive cash, or were you the victim of false privilege or maybe fraud? Progressing to all-time of what extremely happened within the past is that the best method to pass on to an improved future. When rationalization causes real self-delusion and entails blaming others for your own mistakes, or not facing reality, the method becomes a negative one.

In the event of notably severe losses, and even probably with people who don't threaten one's financial survival, there are cases during which individuals suffer from depression or maybe despair. As such, they will resort to those negative brick ways mentioned before, or even worse. In such instances, skilled facilitation is also needed.

Finally, in terms of investing your cash well for the future, it should be valued using the assistance of a freelance monetary consultant with an honest diary record.

The Bottom Line

While changing the past is not possible, you can control how you react to that. Selecting sound ways can assist you to progress quicker and will even assist you to recoup monetary losses.

What are the chances of rating a Winning Trade?

When several people think about chances, the primary

thought that comes to the mind may be a coin toss—having a 50% likelihood of being correct on a given toss, is one thing as straightforward as a coin toss is being applied to finance in money markets.

Probabilities, like a coin toss, will so offer us with tools for approaching the markets and, therefore, the ideas may be applied in additional ways than one would possibly expect. As an example, a trader's read on chance can be fully incorrect, which can be the very reason why they're not creating cash within the markets; this text aims to assist by providing an introduction to the possibilities of commerce and statistics.

Make Sure you have all known before that Coin Toss:

Let's guess that at a specific duration, note a stock may even as simply move up because it could move down (even in a very vary way, stocks move up and down). Thus, our chance of creating a profit on a (short or long) position is 50%, which is the same as a coin flip.

Key Takeaways

• Learning regarding statistics and possibilities will facilitate gauge whether or not returns are possible to continue or if the returns simply happened to flow from a random event.

• A coin flip typically involves mind once considering possibilities, it is a 50% probability that it lands for the first time on the heads and 50% also it can fall on tails.

Options Trading

- The idea of possibilities also can be used as a tool of finance in money markets.

- Determining whether or not superior trading is due to luck or talent typically needs a few years of observation, particularly for longer-term investment ways.

Although most investors wouldn't possibly initiate random short-run trades, we are going to begin within this scenario. If we've got an equal chance of creating a fast profit, will a run of profits or losses signal what future outcomes can be? No! Not on random trades. Every result still features a 50% chance, notwithstanding what outcomes came previously, the similarity is true of a coin toss—if it lands heads 10 consecutive times, the chance of landing on tails on consecutive toss continues to be 50%.

A consecutive streak or a run will happen in random 50:50 events. A run refers to a variety of identical outcomes that occur in a very row. Here may be a table displaying the possibilities of such run; in different words, the percentages of flipping a given variety of heads or tails in a very row, whenever we have a tendency to run into issues. Let's say we've simply created 5 profitable trades in every row per our table, that is giving us the chance of being right (or wrong) 5 times in a very row supported a 50% chance, we've already overcome some serious odds. The percentages of obtaining the sixth profitable trade look extraordinarily remote; however, that's not the case really. Our odds of success are still 50%.

People lose thousands of dollars within the money markets (and in casinos) by failing to understand the randomness of possibilities; the percentages from our coin-toss table are supported by uncertain future events and, therefore, the chance they're going to occur. Once we've completed a run of 5 productive trades, those trades are not any longer uncertain. Our next trade starts a brand new potential run, and when the results are certain every trade, we have a tendency to begin back at the highest of the table; every single time suggests each trade features a 50% likelihood of understanding.

The reason this happens more often is that once traders get into the market, they typically mistake the string of profits or losses as either talent or lack of skill, this is solely not true. Whether or not a short-run dealer makes multiple trades or a capitalist makes solely couple trades each year, we will have to investigate the outcomes of their trades in a totally different method to perceive if they're simply "lucky" or if actual talent is concerned. It's necessary to recollect that statistics apply to all or any timelines.

Long-term Results

The example gave a short-run trade example that supported a 50% likelihood of being right or wrong. However, will this apply to the long term? Noticeably, the explanation is that despite the fact that bargainers could solely take long-run positions, they are going to be doing fewer trades. Thus, this will take longer to achieve data from enough trades to examine if easy luck is concerned or if it had been skill. A short-run dealer could create thirty trades per week and show a profit monthly for 2 years. Has this dealer overcome the percentages with real skill? It appears so because the odds of getting a run of twenty-four profitable months are extraordinarily rare unless the percentages have shifted more within the trader's favor somehow.

What about a long-run investor who has created 3 trades over the last 2 years that have been profitable? Is the bargainer exhibiting skill? Not essentially. Currently, this trader features a run of three going, which isn't tough to accomplish even from wholly random results. The lesson here is that talent isn't simply mirrored within the short-term (whether that's in the future or one year, it'll take issue by trading strategy); it will even be mirrored within the future. You will need enough trade information to accurately verify whether or not a technique is effective enough to beat random chances. And even with this, we have a tendency to face another challenge: whereas every trade is an occasion, therefore maybe a month and year during which trades were placed.

A trader who placed thirty trades per week has overcome the daily odds and, therefore, the monthly odds for a decent variety of periods. Ideally, proving the investment strategy over a couple of more years would erase all doubt that luck was associated due to a particular market condition. For our long-run bargainers building trades that last quite a year, will take several or additional period to prove this particular strategy is beneficial over this long time and the market situation at that specific time or period.

When we think about all timeframes and several market conditions, we start to examine a way to be altogether profitable timeframes and the way to maneuver the percentages often on our facet, attaining larger than a random 50% likelihood of being right. It's worth noting that if profits are larger than losses, a bargainer may be right and is below 50% of the time and still make a profit.

How Profitable Traders Create Cash

Of course, individuals do create cash within the markets, and it's not simply because they need to have a decent run, but they get the percentages in their favor. The profitable results return from 2 different ideals. The primary answer on what was mentioned above—being profitable altogether with timeframes, or a minimum of winning more inbound periods than is lost in others.

Psychological Traps Investors Ought to Avoid

We have so many different authors that have written on psychological or activity traps that have led individuals in the different non-profitable directions not only in trading but also in their lives as a whole. Quite often, some classic kinds of dysfunctional psychological science are directly evident in investment behavior.

Anchoring Trap

First, there's the supposed anchoring lure that refers to an over-reliance on what one originally thinks. Imagine counting on a match and selecting the fighter strictly by who has thrown the foremost punches in their last 5 fights. You'll begin fine by selecting the statistically of the more-active fighter, however, the fighter with the smallest amount of punches could have won 5 bouts by first-round knockouts. Clearly, any metric will become hollow once it's taken out of context.

For instance, if you're thinking that of a precise company as victorious, you'll be too assured that its stocks are an honest bet. This preconception is also altogether incorrect within the prevailing state of affairs or at some purpose in the future.

Take, for example, electronics retailer Radio Shack. One of the thriving sellers of personal electronics and gadgets in the 1980s and 1990s, the chain is crushed by online retailers such as Amazon (AMZN).

Those consigns within that perception that Radio Shack was there to stay lost heaps of cash because the company filed for bankruptcy multiple times and shrinking from its prime size of 7,100 stores to 70 retailers by the end of 2017.

In order to avoid this trap, you wish to stay versatile in your thinking and receptive new sources of data, whereas understanding the fact that any company is often here these days and gone tomorrow. Any manager will disappear too for that matter.

Unsuccessful Price Trap

The unsuccessful price lure is simply as dangerous; this is often regarding psychologically (but not in reality) protective of your previous selections or decisions — that is often fateful for your investments. It is actually arduous to require a loss or settle down for that you just created the incorrect selections or allowed somebody else to form them for you. However, if your investment is not sound enough smart, or sinking quick, the earlier you get out of it and into one thing more brilliant, the better you clung to stocks that you just bought in 1999 at the peak of the *dot.com* boom, you need to have to attend a decade to break even, which is for non-technology stocks. It's much better to not hold tight the unsuccessful price and to urge into alternative asset categories that are moving up quick. Emotional commitment to dangerous investments simply makes things worse.

It is actually arduous to require a loss or settle down for that you just created the incorrect selections or allowed somebody else to form them for you.

Confirmation Lure

Similarly, within the confirmation lure, individuals usually hunt down others who have created and are still creating constant mistakes. Ensure you get objective recommendation from recent sources, instead of consulting the one that gave you the dangerous advice at the first place, if you discover yourself expressing one thing like, "Our stocks have dropped by thirty percent, however, it is sure best simply to hold onto them, isn't it?" So, in this case, it shows that you are looking up for confirmation from another unfortunate capitalist within the similar scenario. You'll be able to comfort one another within the short-run; however, it's simply self-delusion.

Visual Disorder Trap

The situational visual disorder will exacerbate things. Even people who aren't specifically seeking confirmation, usually keep out the prevailing market realities so as to try doing nothing and delay the evil day once the losses just need to be confronted.

If you recognize deep down that there are challenges along with your investments, like a serious scandal at the company or market warnings, or you read everything online aside from the money headlines, then you're most likely tormented by this blinker result.

Theory of Relativity Lure

The theory of relativity trap is additionally there waiting to guide you wide. Everybody incorporates a totally different psychological make-up, combined with a novel set of circumstances extending to work, family, career prospects and certain inheritances. This suggests that though you wish to bear in mind of what others do, their scenario and views aren't essentially relevant outside their own context.

Be aware, however, beware too! You want to invest for yourself and solely in your own context. Your friends could have each the money and therefore the risk-friendliness to speculate inside of pork futures, however, if you're a modest-earning and a nervy person, this is often not for you.

Irrational Exuberance Lure

When investors begin to build your mind to believe that the past equals the future, they're acting as if there's no uncertainty within the market. Sadly, uncertainty never vanishes. There will perpetually be ups and downs, hot stocks, bubbles, mini-bubbles, industry-wide losses, panic marketing in Asia and different unexpected events within the market. Believing that the past predicts the future may be a sign of certainty once enough investors are positive. We've got the conditions of Greenspan's renowned, irrational exuberance, where capitalist certainty pumps the market up to the purpose where a large correction is inevitable. The investors who get hit the toughest — those who are still all-in just before the correction — are the positive ones who are sure that the Bull Run can last forever. Trusting that a bull won't activate you, this is a better way to ensure thanks to getting yourself gored.

Pseudo-Certainty Lure

This phrase shows an investment observation of investors' perceptions as regards to risk. Investors will limit their risk exposure if they assume their portfolio or investment returns are going to be positive – basically protecting the lead – however, they'll ask for additional and more risk if it's like they're heading for a loss.

Basically, investors avoid risk once their portfolios are doing well and will bear more risk once their portfolios are floundering and don't want additional exposure to attainable losses. This is mostly due to the mentality of winning it all back. Investors are willing to boost the stakes to reclaim capital, however, do not produce additional capital for how long would an automobile driver survive if he solely used his brakes once he had the lead.

Superiority Trap

For some individuals, the prevalence trap is extraordinarily dangerous. A lot of investors assume they understand more than the consultants or perhaps the market. Simply being knowledgeable and/or clever doesn't mean you wouldn't need sensible, independent advice. Also, it doesn't mean you'll be able to outgo the professionals and a complex system of markets either. Several investors have lost fortunes through being convinced that they were more knowledgeable than others. Moreover, these individuals are simple prey for some of the rest traps mentioned above.

Conclusion

This brings us to the end of this guide to options trading for beginners. We began by looking at market basics and how price is represented in a chart. Remember that you can use candlestick price formations as a further confirmation for an entry point in your strategies.

For example, if you wish to implement a bear call spread trade, then sighting a pin bar at a major resistance level is a good indicator that price might be about to experience a downswing. Any candlestick pattern you wish to trade must be backed up by an appropriate price environment. For example, sighting a pin bar in the middle of a range or in a small sideways movement in a massive upswing is not a strong sign.

While deciphering price environments is a tough task, you can begin by trading ranges. Ranges tend to be quite stable and their sideways movement ensures that the price will not run away from you, as in trends. Trends will give you the biggest profits, of course, but getting into a trend at the right time is a tough task and more often than not, your entry will be suboptimal.

Options remove this particular problem, thanks to the fact

that you need to pick strike prices, not entry levels as with directional trades. However, begin with ranges and then move forward. Your ability to decipher ranges versus trends is all for naught if you cannot practice proper risk management.

The true measure of risk management is consistency and this involves a lot of things, most of all discipline. It takes discipline to stick to your risk limits per trade and not fall prey to the trap of increasing your risk per trade chasing potential profits. We've seen how the math of your profitability gets skewed when you are inconsistent in this regard.

Your mindset might be at fault if you find it difficult to stay disciplined. A lot of us grow up with toxic ideas of money and success and sometimes, it's easy to view money as the only key to happiness. This puts us in a terrible position when we take a loss, as is inevitable in trading, and puts us in the "all or nothing" type of mindset which is common in academics and usual job scenarios.

Trading is not your usual atmosphere, so it needs to be treated as a business. You need to understand how the odds work and if you keep understanding intellectually how odds work but still get upset over a few lost trades, your mindset is at fault.

Finally, we looked at four profitable options trading strategies which you can implement today. The covered call and the collar are market neutral strategies which will provide you with a decent income per month. Following this, look to implementing the call spread strategies outlined in the final chapter.

There are a number of permutations you can play around with when it comes to the strike prices so keep this in mind when you choose them.

A lot of practice is necessary for you to be successful as a trader so make sure you constantly practice your skills of identifying S/R levels and market environments. Keep practicing and you will get there.

Thank you very much for taking the time to read this book. I'm positive it will help you trade better and more importantly, show you how to make money immediately, almost risk free.

Please do let me know what you think by leaving a review; I'll appreciate it very much!

References

Chen, J. (2019). *Pattern Day Trader Definition.* [online] Investopedia. Available at: https://www.investopedia.com/terms/p/patterndaytrader.asp [Accessed 2 Jul. 2019].

MetaTrader 4. (2015). GlobalPrime.

Tradecity Trading Academy. (2019). *Scientist Discovered Why Most Traders Lose Money - 24 Surprising Statistics - Tradeciety Trading Academy.* [online] Available at: https://www.tradeciety.com/24-statistics-why-most-traders-lose-money/ [Accessed 2 Jul. 2019].